USING MY WORD POWER

Advocating For A More Civilized Society

BOOK II: PATRIOTISM AND POLITICS
REAL ADVOCACY JOURNALISM® Series

JANICE S. ELLIS, Ph.D.

USARiseUp, Inc.

Using My Word Power: Advocating for a More Civilized Society
Book II: Patriotism and Politics
Real Advocacy Journalism® Series

Copyright © 2024 by Janice S. Ellis, Ph.D.

BISAC Codes: 1. POL046000; 2. POL043000; 3. SOC070000; 4. SOC028000; 5. SOC031000

All rights reserved. No part of this publication may be reproduced, distributed, or transmitted in any form or by any means, including photocopying, recording, scanning, or other electronic or mechanical methods without the prior written permission of the publisher or author. For permission requests, contact the publisher or author.

ISBN: 979-8-9878561-4-7 (paperback)
ISBN: 979-8-9878561-5-4 (hardcover)
ISBN: 979-8-9878561-6-1 (digital)

Library of Congress Control Number: 2024921717

Cover design by Lewis Agrell

USARISEUP, Inc.
6320 Brookside Plaza, #275
Kansas City, MO 64213
844-931-2200

https://realadvocacyjournalism.com

Printed in the United States of America

ALSO, BY JANICE S. ELLIS

From Liberty to Magnolia:
In Search of the American Dream (2018)

Shaping Public Opinion:
How *Real Advocacy Journalism*™ Should Be Practiced (2021)

Using My Word Power: Advocating For A More Civilized Society (2022)
Real Advocacy Journalism® Series
Book I: Ethics and Values

From Liberty to Magnolia: In Search of the American Dream—
New Edition (2023)

Dedication

To those who believe in the power of words
to advance a civilized and better society

Reviews and Awards

Excerpts from Reviews Received for Book I in the Using My Word Power Series

The first thing to note about her work is that it comes from the perspective of an active journalist who not only reports on these conditions, but participates in the democratic process of enacting change.

This allows for a more personal and passionate tone that's injected into the mix of reflections, creating an accessible document of American experience that resonates on personal as well as political levels because of this background and focus: *"The writings of an advocate journalist always boil down, directly, or indirectly, intentionally, or unintentionally, to a plea—imploring the reader or listener to think, to consider the facts, the circumstances, the workable solutions for the issues at hand, and when appropriate and necessary to engage in action."*

The book contains commentaries written over the past four decades for radio, a major metropolitan daily newspaper, community newspapers, an online state news publication, and the author's website. The commentaries have been chosen for their timeliness as well as timelessness. They also reflect snapshots of history.

The writings tackle a myriad of evolving situations and present candid analysis that often conclude in a plea for reconsideration on the reader's part:

These wide-ranging questions also emphasize the power of words to outline, convince, and provide alternate perspectives, making these pieces perfect for book clubs, debates, and other interactive forms of dialogue from high school into adult circles.

The result of these works is an effective example of how the written word can change hearts and minds through powerful writing and meaningful discourse.

—D. Donovan, Senior Book Reviewer
Midwest Book Reviews

A veteran writer offers guidance for future advocacy journalists....

Dedicated "to those who believe that our words and actions matter in advancing a more civilized and better society," this book is built on the principle that advocacy journalism is essential to a thriving democracy. With a doctorate in communication arts from the University of Wisconsin, Ellis has an expertise in the field that includes solid academic underpinnings and four decades of experience as an advocacy journalist whose commentary and writings have appeared on radio and blogs and in newspapers. Teaching by example, the book mostly reprints articles that provide readers not only with expert commentary on race relations from the perspective of a Black woman, but also models for neophyte writers. To Ellis, far too many of today's advocacy journalists are willing to sacrifice facts and fairness for partisan propaganda and sensationalism. Alternately, the author implores readers to see advocacy journalism as "a plea" that entreats people "to think, to consider the facts, the circumstances, the workable solutions for the issues at hand, and when appropriate and necessary to engage in action." More than just offering wisdom for today's budding journalists, as a Black writer born in Mississippi who remembers "the humiliation" of segregation firsthand, Ellis gives readers of all vocations a sage voice. She blends solid research with well-reasoned arguments on issues.... The author is a master journalist who skillfully balances her passionate takes with objective facts and effectively deploys "the only real and lasting weapon" people have: their words.

A potent ode to the power of advocacy journalism.

—Kirkus Reviews
The most trusted voice in book reviews since 1933

Using My Word Power: Advocating for a More Civilized Society is a compilation of essays by advocate journalist Janice S. Ellis that prompts the reader to ask: how can we make America a better, stronger nation?

These articles, ranging from as early as 1976 up to recent days, make it clear that disturbingly, in many matters, little has changed in the forty-some years since Ellis's first piece was published. There continues to be gun violence, mass shootings, drug abuse both elicit and prescription, racial violence, and climate change denial. As one essay points out: climate change and racism have in common that some people refuse to believe either exists, despite overwhelming evidence. Each essay has its date revealed only at the end of it, showing that each work could be about the present day.

Using My Word Power is a First Place Award winner of the Nellie Bly Nonfiction Journalism Award.

Janice S. Ellis's work is thoughtful, enlightening and, moreover, timeless. Highly Recommended!

—Chanticleer International Book Reviews

Awards

In addition to the author receiving regional, national, and international awards for her books, she has also received awards for her commentary.

She received the "Best Serious Columnist Award" from the Missouri Press Association during their annual convention in 2023 and 2024.

She also received the "Excellence in Media Award" from the Greater Kansas City Women's Political Caucus at their annual Torch Award ceremony in September 2024.

Her commentaries have appeared in numerous publications across the United States.

Table of Contents

Introduction 1

    Part One: American Ideals and Realities

Prelude: Sample of Earliest Writings ……………....……….....9
      Conserve Energy—An Early Warning
      Trust Between the Community and Law Enforcement
      Is America Experiencing a Moral Crisis
A Tale of Two Families—An American Journey……….........15
Funding Prisons Is a Higher Priority Than
Funding Education in Missouri and Most States. Why?...............19
Affordable Health Care for All……………………..…………… 24
A Democracy Where the Minority Often Rules 27
America Is in a Race to the Bottom……......................…………32
An Unequal Education System for Blacks and Hispanics: Is
This Practice America's Apartheid?..................................……34
America at a Crossroads: Not Voting Is Tantamount to
Being a Citizen AWOL…………………………………………... 38
Are We Reclaiming or Losing What Made America Great?...…....42
Some Defining American Beliefs on Slippery Slope ……… 44
Being President Requires Honesty and Accountability 48
Billboards of President Barack Obama: Disrespectful
and Downright Unpatriotic ……………………………………...51
Beyond September 11 ……………………………………………. 53
Chipping Away of Protected Individual Rights 57
The Church and the Clergy—A Moral, Social and
Political Compass, Still ……………………………………...60
Confederate Statues and Memorabilia Belong in Museums ….....64

Exercising the Basic Right to Vote 67
Focus on the Values That Make America Great 70
Another Fourth of July Holiday—Is It Just About
Fireworks, Picnics, and Parades? 72
Guns in the Hands of Babies...76
Illegal Drugs or Prescription Drugs......................…..............79
In search of America's Voice..............................…..............82
Is America Still a Democratic Republic of the People? 86
How Much Does Racism Influence the Right to Vote? 89
Native American Nicknames and Mascots 93
Las Vegas Killing Spree Was Domestic Terrorism 96
Moving Away From Great Principles That Built America 98
Nationalism Is Surging Amid Unprecedented Globalization 101
On September 11 Americans Became One 104
Removal of Confederate Monuments 106
Role and Responsibility of the Press 108
Selection of Kamala Harris Moves America Forward...............111
Shaping Public Opinion Is An Awesome Responsibility 114
Terrorism Beyond and Within Our Borders 117
The Influence of Religion in American Politics and Public Policy ...120
Who Are We America: Who Are We Becoming? 123
The Popular Vote and the Electoral College 125
Should the President Be America's Role Model ....…......128
The World Is Watching the United States Senate 130
Time to Redefine Domestic Terrorism Regardless of the Motive ... 132
Two Americas Masquerading As One 134
U.S. Treasury Confronts Race and Gender 136
Values and Laws that Make America Great 138
Violence—As American As Apple Pie? 140
What Does the American Dream Mean to You? 143

This Fourth of July Commit to Fight to Save the Soul of America ... 145
Who and What Does America Stand For? 148
Why Is Donald Trump So Appealing? 150
World's Strongest Democracy Tested ………………..……………..153

Part Two: Politics and the People

Prelude: Sample of Earliest Writings……………………………..159
  Politics As a Spectator Sport
Faith Plays An Integral Role in American Politics ……………....161
Negative Political Ads Pollute and Debase the Political
Process of Our Democracy ………………………………………….. 165
New United States Congress Represents US 169
Beware of the Danger of the Undertow 172
Awesome Responsibility of Presidential Leadership ….....……... 176
The People Must Demand Civility From Congress, Now 178
Big Government Bailouts and Big Executive Bonuses:
Longing for the Lessons of Horatio Alger ……………………….... 182
Perils of Not Knowing Your History ……………………………....186
Healthcare Insurance for Millions of Americans at Risk …..…. 188
How Has Electing a Black Man As President
Impacted Race Relations? …………………..……………………190
How Will Trump Govern? …………………………………………193
Coronavirus Is Not Only Infecting and Killing but Exposing …… 195
Coronavirus Should Not Interfere With Elections …………….. 198
Coronavirus Presents Great Opportunities to Become Closer … 201
DACA Exposes the Hypocrisy of Illegal Immigration ………… 204
Do You Approve of What Is Happening in Washington? ……...207
New Alabama Immigration Law Begs for a National Solution … 209
Is Donald Trump a Role Model? …………………………………… 212

Are You in Favor of Passage of the DREAM Act? 214
Playing to Racism: 2012 Presidential Candidates
Missing a Great Opportunity 217
During the 2012 Presidential Election,
the Public Can Just Say "No" 221
Hillary Clinton or Donald Trump? 223
Living In the Moment Can Be Blinding 226
Donald Trump As Role Model 228
Elected Officials Work for You 230
Electing Best Leaders for Times Ahead 234
Continual Erosion of Profile of Political Leaders 238
GOP Wooing Black Voter—Courtship Or Marriage 242
Government Is Big Business:
What Has Your Experience Been Lately? 246
Growing Protest Against Trump 250
Adequate Health Care Coverage:
Too Many Americans Do Not Have It 252
Outcomes of 2020 Elections Will Be Critical 255
Donald Trump Continues to Question
President Obama's Place of Birth 257
Political Leaders of Tomorrow 260
President Trump Is Promoting
Blatant Racism As the New Normal 263
Qualifications to Be President of United States 266
Impeachment Trial Is to Protect the Country 268
Republican Party Has Lost Its Way and Identity .... .271
Republicans Have Themselves to Blame 273
The Obsession With Repealing Obamacare 276
The Congress Christmas Song: Oh, You'd Better Watch Out 279

To Impeach Or Not to Impeach Is the Question 283
Toward a More Diverse Peace Corps 286
Trump Is Many Americans' Alter Ego 289
Trump Hurls Insults Instead of Debating 292
Donald Trump, Truth, and Consequences 295
Partisanship Trumps Public Policy ....…....................... 298
Show Real Patriotism by Voting 301
Your Vote Is a Terrible Thing to Waste 305
Will the Republican Party Recover? 309
Elected Officials Work for Us.
What Criteria Should We Use to Hire Them? 312

Postscript: Onward and Upward 317

Sources ………………………………………………………...319

About the Author…………………………………………..... 321

Note: The reviews, introduction, and the author's biographical information contain excerpts from Book I in the Real Advocacy Journalism® series because of factual inherency. The collection of commentaries listed above is unique to Book II. The author maintains all rights.

Introduction

I have been an advocate journalist for more than four decades. I have always felt I was born, reared, and came of age during a very pregnant and poignant time not only in an evolving America, but an evolving society.

From poverty's perch, farm life, family and the confining community in which I grew up, I found my sense of purpose and determination to try to change things, to make them better. I managed to achieve the pinnacle in graduate education. I have had a successful career in both the private and public sectors.

As life has had its way, I have loved and lost, given birth and reared children alone, weathered verbal and physical abuse from trusted lovers, recovered from colossal failures—all while navigating American life, as a woman, black, or as a black and a woman (whichever comes into play), forever fighting against allowing either of those indelible birthmarks to define me, or confine me. More about the trials and triumphs of my life are described in my memoir, *From Liberty to Magnolia: In Search of the American Dream* (2018).

As circumstances, issues, and forces—social, political, economic—occur all around me, push against me, I have chosen to push back. I have consciously entered and continue to enter the fray, using the power of words—the only real and lasting weapon I have.

Being a journalist has not been my formal training nor my profession. Becoming an advocate journalist has been my calling. I have always, since leaving graduate school and seeking to find my productive place in society, kept pen and paper—now a smartphone or notepad—near to capture an idea, a thought, or a plea, regarding some human condition, some public policy issue, or some social problem. I have even written complete commentary on cocktail napkins during a return flight from a business trip, after having put my briefcase or computer in the overhead bin. I dared not to have taken the chance to retrieve either and run the risk of losing the idea, the message, more a plea, which beckoned to be expressed.

The writings of an advocate journalist always boil down, directly or indirectly, intentionally or unintentionally, to a plea—imploring the reader or listener to think, to consider the facts, the circumstances, the possible solutions for the issues at hand, and when appropriate and necessary, to act.

While being a woman, a black, a wife, a mother, a career professional, and carrying out my calling to be an advocate journalist, I have primarily addressed some of the most enduring issues of our times. But also, I could not ignore the temporal—pressing issues of the hour. Most of my writings over the decades have maintained their relevancy, fulfilling a needed voice albeit often crying in a wilderness or falling on deaf ears and blind eyes. One of my newspaper editors characterizes my commentaries as "evergreens." For that I am grateful. That characterization has kept me writing when in those infrequent moments I have thought, "Why am I bothering to write anything?"

During the past four decades, the commentaries have been written for a large radio station, a major metropolitan daily newspaper, community newspapers, as a guest columnist for a metropolitan business journal, and currently online.

Throughout, I have tried to adhere to the standards of what I call *Real Advocacy Journalism*®, which is the subject of my award-winning book, *Shaping Public Opinion: How Real Advocacy Journalism*™ *Should Be Practiced* (2021), and is covered in detail. But in sum, much of the advocacy journalism practiced today is partisan, biased, and often blurs the lines between truth and lies, facts and fiction, and often presents fake news as real news. The purpose and objectives of such advocacy journalism constitute propaganda to gain public support for the interest and agenda of an individual, a powerful few, a special interest group, or a small constituency rather than for the good of the majority.

In my writings, I have endeavored to apply the principles and tenets of *Real Advocacy Journalism*®, which is to stick to the facts, analyze them, put an event, situation, or issue into perspective in order to foster a better understanding, and provide direction to form an opinion or pursue an action. We all live and function in an orbit of influence. How in depth a particular commentary addresses a subject matter was determined by the time allotted for the radio spot, the space in a newspaper, or word count online.

I do not proclaim that each and every one of my commentaries have been exhaustive on a particular subject or met all the noble standards of *Real Advocacy Journalism*®. But adhering to those standards in providing a meaningful perspective has always been my goal.

In surveying my writings over the decades, their focus can be organized in three categories: Ethics and Values; Justice and Equality; and Patriotism and Politics, and I have compiled them in three books accordingly.

This is Book II, Patriotism and Politics, of three books in the *Real Advocacy Journalism*® series. Book I, Ethics and Values (2022) and Book III, Justice and Equality (2025) are also under the title *Using My Word Power: Advocating for a More Civilized Society*.

In each book, the commentaries have been grouped under major section headings. I have begun each section with one of the very first commentaries that were written and delivered in a 2-minute spot on WISN radio, the largest ABC affiliate, located in Milwaukee, Wisconsin during 1974-76 to show how their subject area and treatment still resonate today. All commentaries, written across the decades, have been chosen for their enduring relevancy in terms of the *timeliness* and *timelessness* of their subject matter—then and now. Many represent historical accounts of defining moments, incidents, and issues that have had lasting impact on, and lessons learned about American society.

Following the initial two years of delivering commentaries on WISN radio, columns have been written for newspapers over three decades. During the last ten years, and today, they primarily appear online. All commentaries published online at JaniceSEllis.com and the MissouriIndependent.com contain evidentiary links that are inaccessible in the printed version but can be accessed in the digital versions of the books. The dates and where the commentaries appeared/appear are found at the end of each.

My hope is that in sharing my attempts to improve understanding about issues that impact us all that you will be informed, enlightened, inspired and have reaffirmation that in addition to our beliefs, our words and actions are what advances a more civilized and better society.

Part One

American Ideals and Realities

America, the Republic with a democratic form of government—while at once an ideal and reality, and while at once united and divided—has managed to survive and thrive for nearly 250 years. As a collective where individual rights are vehemently valued and protected, many inherent and emerging challenges are addressed, and often they are ignored. This collection of commentaries addresses many of those social, educational, and political issues across race, age, gender, and socioeconomic status. My hope is to illustrate how we can use our voice to bring about needed and meaningful dialogue that results in changes for the better.

Prelude: Sample of Earlier Writings

Conserve Energy—An Early Warning

Despite all the warnings, all the statistics, and the continual rising cost of fuel, the necessity of conserving energy still has not been impressed upon Americans to any significant degree. No major changes in lifestyles can be detected.

Sure, there are a few of us who have chosen to ride in a carpool or take the bus rather than drive our own car. But if you look at the lanes adjacent to you as you drive on the freeway, you can readily tell that not enough of us have chosen to ride in a carpool.

Then there are other things which can be done by individuals to conserve energy, but are we doing them?

How many of us make sure we are not using electricity needlessly with excessive lighting—having lamps and lights on when they are not in use?

The same is true of appliances and electrical tools. We let them run during the interim they are not in use.

USING MY WORD POWER

Many of us will let the radio or television play simply to provide "noise" in the background. Oftentimes, we are not listening, watching, or attending in any way.

How many of us will keep our homes at a temperature between 68 and 70 degrees this winter?

I dare many of us to take inventory of how we use energy during the course of a given day. We are likely to find that we waste a great deal. The crucial consideration is: Once we determine how we are wasting energy, will that be enough to encourage us to stop? Or will it take some natural disaster to make us see the need to conserve the limited supply of energy we have left.

It wasn't that long ago that we were faced with the rationing of gasoline, increases in the price of all kinds of fuel, and mandatory speeds on the nation's highways. And, it wasn't that long ago that we met long lines at some service stations, and closed doors at others.

We will do well to remember as we consume energy daily that our supply is limited and that the next time the energy panic button is pushed, we may have to deal with more drastic measures for a longer period of time.

Delivered August 7, 1976
WISN Radio, ABC Affiliate

Trust Between the Community and Law Enforcement

Many Milwaukee citizens are losing confidence in the law enforcement process. The skepticism is a result of the way inquests are handled after a suspected criminal is fatally shot by police.

Whenever someone is fatally shot, there is confusion about whether an inquest will be held at all. State law requires the district attorney to order an inquest when circumstances surrounding a death indicate there could have been a law violated on the part of those who are supposed to be enforcing the law. The local district attorney's office has also stated at one point that an inquest can be ordered anytime it is requested by a relative of a victim.

Why can't ordering an inquest be automatic whenever a policeman is involved in a fatal shooting, whether clearly in self-defense or under unclear circumstances? This would settle the suspicions in citizens' minds that a cover-up could be taking place behind closed doors. This would help dispel the belief that police often use force unjustifiably.

The community needs to feel that it can trust the police to protect it from those who might bring physical harm to its people and its property. But the community must also be able to feel that the police will be fair in doing so, using no more force than necessary. A public inquiry is a way of laying everything on the table.

In the long run, everybody is better off: The relatives of the victim will feel that justice was done even if the outcome was tragic, and a healthy relationship between police officers and the community can still be one of mutual trust and respect.

The community and law enforcement need each other to promote and maintain a safe environment.

Delivered on September 3, 1975
WISN Radio, ABC Affiliate

Is America Experiencing a Moral Crisis?

There is growing concern among social scientists that America may be experiencing a "moral crisis." Many individuals no longer have the accepted standard of moral conduct they once had to guide their moral and ethical choices, and more than ever before the burden is on the individual to make his or her own decisions as to what is right or wrong.

We have only to momentarily reflect on the realization that over the past several years we have been exposed to the themes of sex, violence, and other areas of moral conduct at an unprecedented rate. Ten or 15 years ago, a highly publicized convention of prostitutes would have been unheard of. Yet several months ago prostitutes met to organize and demand "hookers' rights."

Currently, there is a book on the market in which 28 well-known Americans tell of their first sexual experience, and of course, we all remember the controversial interview with Betty Ford where she discussed sexual and moral issues as they might affect the First Family.

These examples show how certain subjects, once forbidden to be mentioned publicly, are now common conversation topics to be discussed freely and candidly. What is not readily seen is the moral dilemma in which such openness might put an individual. Often, following the discussion, an individual is left to form his or her own opinion and make life-changing or life-altering decisions. The problem comes when the individual is not prepared to make such decisions, either because of a lack of emotional maturity or a lack of a full understanding of the potential consequences of one's choices.

The individual finds himself or herself wandering aimlessly, searching for a suitable lifestyle as he/she experiments with various alternatives, many of which are harmful and leave indelible scars. Interestingly enough, this "openness" or "permissiveness" on the part of society has not decreased the rate of mental illness or suicide. In fact, many social scientists fear that new freedoms of speech and discussion have driven both rates up. The same can be said for other social problems such as alcoholism, violent crime, sexual crimes, divorce, and the like.

To reevaluate social values and morals is a healthy endeavor. But to create a situation where the quality of life deteriorates because of a lack of clearly defined values or moral paths is tragic.

Where are we going, America?

Delivered on March 14, 1976
WISN Radio, ABC Affiliate

A Tale of Two Families—An American Journey

As we come to the close of black history month, it might serve us well to pause and put a few things in perspective if we ever hope to achieve a society where there will be no need for a black history month. When we will no longer need to have a special designation to celebrate the contributions of any race or ethnic group.

But rather, we will have arrived at a point where we chronicle and commemorate the contributions of all Americans in the same history books. We pass on to our families around the dinner table the rich, diverse, and complete American story—in all of its shame, its beauty, and its glory.

Sadly, that day is not today. So, we must prod on.

But how can we ever expect to make a *real* change in how we perceive, understand, and relate to each other if we are not willing to look at where we are today and the reasons why we are there. That will require an open mind and some painful admissions on all of our parts about the American family unit—both black and white.

The black and white family's journey has been different. One of privilege. The other of paucity. One family has typically emerged out of a history where the presence of both parents has been valued and promulgated; the other family from an institution of slavery that raped and destroyed the family unit, separating mother and father, mother, and child. One family has been able to move within society with what appears to be automatic acceptance; the other constantly facing rejection either blatantly or subtly.

One family is afforded a certain level of economic prosperity; the other often denied, limited, or trapped in a perpetual cycle of poverty. One family is exposed and provided with the highest quality of educational training; the other subjected to sub-standard learning environments. One family lives in a neighborhood absent from blight and crime, the other constantly plagued by it.

And yet, we wonder why.

Black folks wonder why some white teenagers from wealthy and not-so wealthy neighborhoods choose to build bombs and go on shooting rampages and kill fellow classmates, teachers, and family members. White folks wonder why some black teenagers would rather sell drugs, shoot a fellow teenager for money or a jacket and rob the elderly.

Black folks wonder why any able-bodied white person needs to be on welfare when they have an easier time getting gainfully employed than their black counterparts. White folks think there are more able-bodied black folks getting a free ride on the welfare rolls than there are whites.

Black folks think affirmative action and set-asides are needed to level the playing field. White folks think such measures reverse discrimination.

And there are those black and white folks who think none of the above. They understand that we all are the sum total of our experience and that begins and is shaped by the family unit of which we are a part. They have immovable faith in the human will and spirit to overcome adversity and impoverished conditions. They fervently believe that someday race will not define how we see each other, or how well we work to build stronger families for a better America through better education, gainful employment, quality housing, good neighborhoods, and other supportive services. Through the transmission of good values.

There are black folks and white folks who recognize that the family unit holds the key. It must be strong. It must be healthy.

Irrespective of the situations in which we find ourselves—some we share as black and white families other we do not—they did not come about overnight. Our children, and their actions good or bad, represent the culmination of values, beliefs, practices, and conditions passed from one generation to another.

The American family unit—black or white—in all its forms is at a precarious time in its history. While some have been blessed with privilege, and others plagued and imperiled by paucity, promoting the health and wellbeing

USING MY WORD POWER

of all families, ultimately, holds the cure.
   We no longer need to wonder why.

Published February 22, 2000
The Kansas City Star

Funding Prisons Is a Higher Priority Than Funding Education in Missouri and Most States. Why?

In America, the land of the free, there are more prisons and more prisoners than any other country in the world. This is not a new phenomenon. For decades, the rate of imprisonment in the United States has been more than twice that of its nearest developmental counterpart.

The long-standing question, both at home and abroad, is: Why is the prison population so high?

One could argue it is to sustain a substitute institution of enslavement built on systemic denial of opportunity and disenfranchisement.

There are many reasons given, like waging a war on illegal drugs and overall increases in various crime rates. But such answers do not get at the root causes and perpetuation of the nearly $200 billion mass incarceration industry that fuels the economy of states across America.

One must look at who makes up the prison populations across states and why. Pick any state—your state—and you will find Blacks make up disproportionately the highest rate of people in prison. For example, in Missouri, black people make up 12% of the state's population, but 34% of the people in prison.

Overall, in America, Blacks are only 13.4% of the total U.S. population. They make up nearly 40% of the prison population. Why are there more Blacks in prisons in America?

In every aspect of American life, Blacks continue to suffer or be victimized disproportionately. This has been the case since the founding of this country, after the abolishment of slavery, and even after the passage of Constitutional Amendments supposedly to make all things equal.

Blacks have been and continue to be denied equal access to a quality education, jobs, housing, health care services and other privileges afforded other Americans.

What has been the results? A debilitating and destructive state of poverty, delinquency and under achievement, which often result in a perpetual cycle of crime and incarceration.

Let's look at the cycle of how Blacks end up in prison more than any other group in America. It begins in grade school with Blacks being disciplined and expelled at higher rates than other students.

Blacks make up 15% of all public school students but are 39% of those suspended or expelled from school.

A PBS New hour segment, a few years ago, highlighted a report that found that suspension and expulsion rates for Blacks were significantly higher than those of whites in 13 southern states. What is that reminiscent of?

The way the suspensions and expulsions of blacks are handled, often engaging law enforcement agencies, has created a practice called the school-to-prison pipeline, according to an investigation conducted by the Ash Center at the Harvard Kennedy School.

Missouri is one of the worst states engaging in this practice, suspending more Black preschooler than 44 other states.

There are trends that show a direct correlation between suspensions, expulsions, failure to complete high school and high incarceration rates. Those children are the same struggling academically and have disciplinary issues.

Yet, the growing practice across America is to invest more into building new prisons or renovating older ones rather than investing in schools and educational support programs. This is tantamount to prejudging and presentencing children who could benefit from meaningful intervention programs.

Another study found that almost every state spends much more money per prisoner than money per student in public schools.

Missouri spends $10,810 per student in 2021, and was spending $22,187 per inmate in 2015.

Just recently, the governor of Arkansas announced that the state is allocating $6 billion to build new prisons and renovate older ones. New prisons will also be built in New Mexico, Oklahoma and South Dakota.

The Alabama legislature passed bills and the governor signed them into law that will use up to $400 million of

Covid-19 relief funds from the federal government to build new prisons and renovate others.

There seems to be no priority for funding education, prevention, and rehabilitation programs.

Where are the announcements from states about the millions of dollars they will be investing in early childhood education and educational programs to close the achievement gaps of the underprivileged, those likely to end up in the penal system?

Low-income, impoverished communities in the Black urban cores across America suffer most from the lack of or underinvestment in educational resources and programs.

It seems that state leaders and legislatures would rather plan, build, and invest in a future of imprisonment than one of accomplishment for our children, particularly Black children, perpetuating a profitable industry on the misfortunes cause by centuries of denial and gross disparities.

Over the decades there has been an acute awareness and discussion about the educational achievement gap between Blacks and whites. But what has been done about it?

While there have been some efforts to close the educational divide, major gaps still remain in basic areas such as proficiency in reading, writing and math skills. The gap is even wider when it comes to technology. Becoming technologically proficient is critical now and will be more so in the future.

Many Black children do not have adequate access to computers or Internet connectivity. This proved to be a major impediment to virtual learning during the height of Covid-19 when most schools were closed.

Better access to educational resources to ensure achievement is a great path toward prevention and breaking the devastating school-to-prison pipeline practice.

The pipeline is bolstered by the fact that Blacks received longer and harsher sentences than whites for the same crimes and the recidivism rate is higher.

One could conclude that failure to invest in quality education is just another way to silently guarantee that the mass incarceration industry will continue to thrive by using a revolving door of suspensions, expulsions, prison terms, and prison returns.

What will it take to change the priority from funding prisons to funding education to minimize, if not stop, the self-perpetuating cycle of crime and loss of freedom?

Published October 18, 2021
Missouri Independent.com

Affordable Health Care for All

What is the problem with providing affordable health care for all, blacks, whites, rich and poor?

The Affordable Care Act has had and could continue to have an impact on your ability to access the health care services needed whether you are white, black, brown, or yellow. Obamacare, as the policy has been labeled, seeks to significantly increase the number of Americans who will have health care coverage.

Isn't that a positive, a good thing? If not, why not?

The sad fact is access to adequate health insurance coverage is still out of reach for tens of millions of Americans. However, ever since the passage of the Affordable Care Act, there has been non-stop partisan clamor to repeal it. Suits have been filed against it.

And now the newly elected Republican leadership of both houses of Congress is threatening to repeal, dismantle, gut, or undo The Affordable Care Act in one way or another. It is also likely to go before the Supreme Court once again in an effort to gut its key provisions.

What is most at stake is the provision that mandates all individuals to get some type of health insurance.

What is wrong with that provision? Isn't having car insurance a requirement by law?

The bill has many important provisions, among them not allowing discrimination of those who might have a pre-existing condition, no co-pay costs for seeking preventive care, allowing children to stay on their parent's policy until age 25, a great value for those college years. There are other provisions needed.

Evidence abounds that we all pay—one way or the other—when emergency rooms and urgent care centers are filled with patients who either have limited or no insurance at all. They do not have the means to access preventive or primary care, preventing a minor illness from becoming a catastrophic incident or an acute episode becoming a chronic disease.

So why wouldn't there be policy measures to not only provide health care services for most Americans, but also try to identify and manage continuing spiraling health care costs?

It is not a secret who makes up the uninsured in this country. Blacks, Hispanics, low-income whites, and their children make up the greatest number.

All of these people are not on welfare. Many work two jobs to make ends meet. The problem is that many have jobs that do not offer health insurance as a benefit. So, the hard worker not only works hard but also cannot afford a day off if he/she becomes sick. So often, acute, and minor health problems turn into chronic and catastrophic diseases.

There are also long-term, cyclical consequences. Among the many challenges poorer children face every day, imagine them performing at their best in school when they are not feeling well, and their parents cannot afford a doctor's visit or the medications to knock out a common childhood infection or illness. Imagine the unnecessary suffering among poor elderly.

While we are still in an anemic, yet recovering economy, America is still one of the richest nations on earth. It begs the question why so many Americans lack adequate health care coverage? And why was there such a partisan political divide to try and find a solution that had both positive humanitarian and fiscal outcomes?

Making a concerted effort to reduce the number of uninsured and underinsured should be a part of the legislative agenda at all levels of government.

Should the Republican Congress or Supreme Court strike down Obamacare, every American should demand of their elected official specifics about what will be put in its place. Listen carefully to their answers.

What is their plan for making health care coverage available for tens of millions of Americans?

Do not accept a Nonanswer. The health of too many Americans, present and future generations, is at stake.

Published November 21, 2014
https://janicesellis.com/blog

A Democracy Where the Minority Often Rules

America's form of democracy supposed to be one where the consent of the majority rules. But is it?

This question could not resonate any louder than when it comes to passing sensible gun control measures to stop the mass killing of unsuspecting citizens with military style weapons.

The devastating tragedy in Uvalde, Texas, where the lives of 19 elementary school children and two adult were brutally taken a mere 10 days following the supermarket mass shooting in Buffalo, New York, where 10 unsuspecting shoppers were murdered.

Those incidents made worldwide news. Sadly, mass shootings occur all too often. As of this writing, 20 more have occurred since Uvalde, making a total of 243 mass shootings in the United States this year. More shootings than the days so far.

In addition to the lost lives and physical injuries, the effects of these senseless killings on families and communities where they occur are lifelong.

In the meantime, many of us are left wondering when or where the next carnage will occur.

Yet, the majority of Americans have made it clear that they want sensible gun control measures put into place. Measures like universal background checks, banning military style weapons, gun buy-back programs and red flag laws.

Is the minority or the majority controlling legislative actions or inaction when it comes to passing sensible gun control measures?

Is America's form of democracy one where the minority rules?

Yes, most citizens are free to vote for who will represent them. Indeed, the majority determines who will hold various legislative offices.

But whether voting for a person to represent you, or voting for an initiative petition, are the election results, alone, democracy at work? Once the person you voted for gets into the office, does he or she actually represent your interests in the legislative halls? When a majority of citizens vote for a particular initiative petition, is it implemented as approved?

These are questions worth asking. But it doesn't stop there.

What about when a majority of citizens polled make it clear that they prefer the president, Congress and state legislatures to take a particular course of action?

In critical areas, it seems that the will of the majority has little value and is repeatedly ignored. What's worse is that many elected officials are comfortable doing so time after time.

Perhaps, the most egregious and depraved example is the cowardice and constant failure of elected officials to pass sensible measures to minimize, if not stop, the carnage that takes the lives of innocent people.

Other countries have done it, but not the United States.

How many more incidents will it take for the United State Senate to pass sensible gun control measures to stop the horrid massacre of school children?

But gun control is not the only issue where the will of the majority is ignored.

At the national level, the majority of Americans do not think the U.S. Supreme Court should overturn Roe vs. Wade and that women should have access to legal abortions.

A majority of Americans are in favor of universal health care. The Affordable Care Act, also known as Obamacare, has had legislative and legal opposition that reached the Supreme Court. And partisan politics still pledge to continue the fight to undo it, putting millions of Americans at risk of losing healthcare coverage

At the state level, Missouri lawmakers opposed Medicaid expansion. The issue was put on the ballot and ultimately approved by voters. The state legislature continued to fight or delay implementing it.

Even the most obvious tenet of democracy, where the will of people can be determined —the vote — is under siege. Efforts in many states are being initiated to make it more difficult to determine the will of the majority.

USING MY WORD POWER

Is America merely masquerading as a democracy of the people, by the people and for the people?

It seems that, too often, the will of the majority stops at the ballot box. Once elected officials get into office, more attention is paid to the lobbyists, special interests and those who provided the largest financial contributions to their campaigns, or some partisan agenda of a minority.

Money and minority interests seem to trump the will of the majority of citizens who voted to elect them.

But we, the majority, are not without blame. Too many of us are content and see voting as our primary role to ensure that democracy works.

Casting a vote is only the beginning. We must do more to monitor the actions and hold accountable those we elect to do what is in the best interests of our community and family. When they don't, we need to vote them out of office.

Such monitoring and accountability must occur at every level of government.

Otherwise, representative government that supposed to carry out the will of the majority will continue to be ignored, marginalized, and discarded.

We are confronted yet again with an issue where majority will seems not to matter —addressing continual availability of military style guns that are used in mass killings and injuries of innocent Americans, in public places that were once deemed safe if not sacred.

Why would the majority continue to let the minority rule, and allow our elected officials in Congress and our states to merely lob an opening salvo instead of passing meaningful legislation to control gun violence?

While we sit idlily by the carnage continues.

Published June 6, 2022
Missouri Independent.com

America Is in a Race to the Bottom

America is in a race to the bottom when it comes to doing what it takes to clean up our environment and reduce climate change.

With the United States' recent withdrawal for the Paris Climate Accord, where over 200 countries agreed to do something to reduce air pollution, America is in a race to the bottom. This move puts us in the same group as Syria and Nicaragua. America is now lumped with Syria and Nicaragua? Really?

When it comes to nations committing to do what they can to stop global warming, and reduce toxic emissions into Earth's fragile atmosphere, the United States should be leading the way. The U.S. has the largest carbon footprint of all the nations that signed on to the Paris Climate Accord.

Our way of life—gas and oil usage in our modes of transportation, our use and improper disposal of plastics and aerosol products, to name a few—our overall fossil fuel consumption is doing the most damage to the Earth's environment.

Yet, President Trump has gone ahead and announced that the U.S. is pulling out of the Climate Accord. This indicates America will not be held accountable to do all it can to save our planet for our children, grandchildren, great grandchildren—not only our posterity, but humankind.

Once a world leader in so many areas, America is in a race to the bottom when it comes to caring for and protecting planet Earth.

America became a leader nation because of its Democratic principles, and individual rights that go hand-in-hand with a free capitalistic entrepreneurial society. But, when saving or making more money for a few people trumps doing the best for a healthy quality life for all humanity, then it is time to recognize how far out of balance America has become.

It is time to ask, what values do we as Americans hold dear. Are any of those values sacrosanct? Or are we willing to do what seems to be financially expedient regardless of the negative consequences short and long term?

Choosing to ignore and distort the scientific facts about global warming, climate change, and the dangers of an atmosphere laden with pollutants will not "make America great again."

America is in a race to the bottom among its long-standing allies and most other nations on Earth, except Syria and Nicaragua, when it comes to cleaning up our environment.

As Americans, do we care?

June 15, 2017
https://janicesellis.com/blog

An Unequal Education System for Blacks and Hispanics: Is This Practice America's Apartheid?

Another study has once again confirmed that there is a pervasive practice in schools across America where blacks, Hispanics and poor children are consistently denied access to and an equal opportunity to achieve a quality education. This translates into a situation where those who need a good education the most to improve their quality of life and reach their potential are relegated to a social and economic state from which they can never escape.

The most recent study to be released this week is one that was conducted by the Schott Foundation about the nation's largest public school system—the New York City public schools.

The study, "A Rotting Apple: Education Redlining in New York City," confirms that there is an inequitable distribution of educational resources at every level, including the most important resource of all, qualified and experienced teachers, among blacks and Hispanic students and children who are poor. This results in these children having a slim to none chance of learning the skills needed to succeed in anything. They certainly have little chance of graduating with the requisite skills to go to college, a trade school or get a decent job.

The study shows that the evidence of inequities and sub-standard educational practices is blatant and seems to be an acceptable norm. "Unequal learning opportunities for poor students and students of color have become the status quo in New York City," according to John Jackson, president of the Schott Foundation.

Jackson goes on to say that, "The current policy landscape in New York does very little to give these young people access to support, types of schools or experienced teachers that give them a substantive opportunity to learn. We need creative leadership to promote greater equity and alignment, so the city no longer relegates our neediest children to the most troubled schools with the most limited resources, thereby limiting their potential for future success."

But creative leadership must be coupled with real contrition about this shameful practice and real resolve to not stop working for change until oppression in education is abolished right here on American soil.

The tragedy in it all is that the Schott Foundation's study confirms in New York City public schools what a recent national study reveals about this practice happening in schools all across America.

The recent nationwide K-12 Data Collection report conducted by the U.S. Department of Education's civil rights office paints a dismal and disturbing picture of how blacks and Hispanic students are treated in the nation's schools—unfortunately, the majority of the nation's schools. The data was collected from more than 72,000 schools that represent 85 percent of all students.

This study also shows that black and Hispanic students are put on a track of underachievement. In addition to not having quality, experienced and well-paid teachers, these students are in classrooms where the educational materials, tools, technology, and other resources are inadequate, outdated, and insufficient. The report highlights that a high percentage of teachers in schools with the highest black and Hispanic enrollment had taught two years or less. Those teachers are also paid significantly less than their counterparts in other schools.

What has really been achieved since the history-changing case of Brown vs. The Board of Education, which supposedly was the beginning of discrimination ending in education decades ago? How is it, with the 21st Century facing some of its greatest societal challenges we are still tolerant, still willing to turn a blind eye toward an educational system that does not create equal opportunities for all of our children?

How do we expect to break the cycle of poverty and underachievement, crime-ridden neighborhoods, un and underemployment, hopelessness, and resignation to second, third, fourth class citizenship right here in America if we continue to allow an educational caste system to prevail?

What lessons can America take from all of the countries that are doing a better job of educating their children with an education that surpasses us in quality and competitiveness.

If we continue to be stuck on caste and color in this country, it will be our undoing as other countries not only gain the edge but surpass us.

Are we letting the old vestiges of racism reign? It may have worked in the past centuries. It will not continue to work and propel us forward in centuries to come.

Why can't we as Americans not realize that?

Published April 20, 2012
USAonRace.com

America At a Crossroads: Not Voting Is Tantamount to Being a Citizen AWOL

Not voting in the 2012 presidential primary elections is tantamount to an act of cowardice. At a bare minimum, it certainly can be considered laziness. What is the difference between being a *nonvoter* in a democracy and a *deserter* in the military? They both represent dereliction of duty.

Failing to vote is cowardice because it shows a lack of courage to take a stand, work, and vote for one party or the other and its candidates. It is laziness because it shows a lack of energy to invest the time to understand the positions and differences among the choices in order to make an informed decision on Election Day.

Cowardice and laziness seem especially fitting when we are likely to face some of the most important and closest races in recent history—when every eligible voter needs, and should want, to be counted. America in many ways is at a critical crossroads.

While all attention is being focused on the undecided voters, something needs to be done to prick the conscience of the nonvoters. *Nonvoters* have become comfortable being non-entities—not counted—relying on others to make the decision, only to become chronic complainers.

There are growing reasons to be alarmed. There was a time when *nonvoters* would have been too ashamed to admit they did not vote or were not registered. But, today, many claim their non-participation with comfort and ease—seemingly to wear it as a badge of non-patriotic honor.

You can almost hear their pious boastings: "Voting for those incompetent crooks is beneath me. Politics and government are no longer honorable professions." While the current Congress has one of the lowest approval ratings in recent history, it is still no excuse.

Brash, non-voting braggarts, too many of us have become.

What a way to demonstrate being a proud American, thankful to those who made it possible, many by giving their lives for the democratic principles they fervently believed in, including the right to vote.

More and more, we are squandering the privilege with no shame, no remorse, and no sense of obligation or responsibility. Very little connection is made between failing to vote and the quality of one's family life, the well-being of one's community, the quality of neighborhood schools, availability of jobs, and the buying power of a hard-earned dollar.

How will our democratic process survive if this downward spiral of non-voting continues? If fewer and fewer Americans vote, over time what kind of democracy will there be?

Many young people offer such frivolous reasons as politics is boring, irrelevant, or uninteresting. Many older people hide behind cynicism, finding fault, placing blame as solace is found in self-righteous indignation and the ignoble position of being a *nonvoter*.

Candidates can work tirelessly to earn the right to hold an office to serve their country and the people they represent. Our political process is not a one-way street. Its failure or success is not left solely up to the candidates.

There will be Presidential primary elections and other local elections held until November 2012. Candidates for these offices present clear and distinct choices. If you are claiming there is no difference between Newt Gingrich, Mitt Romney, Ron Paul, or Rick Santorum, you are truly out of touch with your government and its future impact on your life and the lives of your loved ones.

Voting is a small investment that yields decisive consequences in the quality of life in America, in your state, in your city, in your community, and the overall quality of our democratic process.

If the shoes of spinelessness and being trifling don't fit you, then don't wear them. One must ask, however, "If it were up to nonvoters, where would our governmental process be?"

The morning after any election of which you could have been apart, will your action have demonstrated concern or a cop-out?

Published January 31, 2012
USAonRace.com

Are We Reclaiming or Losing What Made America Great?

When you tune in to the news, is what you are seeing and hearing consistent with the values that defined or will continue to define America? Are we reclaiming or losing what made America great?

One could argue that the apparent increase in blatant racial and ethnic intolerance, hatred, and inequality have always been a part of America. Indeed, racial injustices are interwoven throughout America's history. But were we not getting better? Were racial and ethnic relations improving?

What has made so many, so comfortable to speak, demonstrate, assault, even kill fellow Americans solely because of racial hatred, much of which is sadly ill-conceived, ill-founded, and based on downright lies and misrepresentations. That is the tragedy in it all.

With this kind of spurious and scurrilous speech and behavior, are we reclaiming or losing what made America great?

One must ask why the atmosphere in America is so toxic, not with the harmful chemical spewing from our consumption habits, but because of the constant flow of lies, gross misrepresentations, and propaganda coming from public leaders whose sole purpose is to divide and change America for the worse.

Every day, every news cycle, irrespective of where you turn, contains comments and actions that are so un-American, so different from the America that has taken pride in marching toward respect, equal opportunity, and equal rights for all of its citizens.

If the leaders of this nation are doing things that are contrary to the values that made America a good nation, how can we be marching toward greatness?

There is a lot about America that needs fixing. The area of immigration seems to be the one getting all of the attention during the past months and apparently the foreseeable future. But must we resort to extreme speech and inhuman actions, even inaction, in trying to fix it? Are such actions making America great?

Are you proud of the speech, actions, and behavior of your elected officials, who are functioning on your behalf? Do they represent you and your values? Do they engender pride in you and make you feel proud to be an American?

We the people, with our speech, with our actions, are we reclaiming or losing what made America great?

In the coming mid-term elections, commit to vote for those who support your values, who support what is good for America and all Americans.

Published June 30, 2018
https://janicesellis/blog

Some Defining American Beliefs on Slippery Slope

Many basic values, principles and practices that built America are in a state of serious decline because of our growing willingness to tolerate almost anything in the name of freedom and free expression.

This unbridled tolerance is exacting a very high price, and it will continue until we reclaim the proven premise that a strong democracy depends upon embracing and upholding certain moral truths. Democracy and morality go hand in hand.

But it seems that democracy and morality are in a growing tug of war. Some of us are quick to think any insistence on the adherence to some moral truths is a threat to individual freedom.

So, in the name of freedom, we are both active and passive participants in the decline of American civil society. The decline, and eventual demise, of a civilized society is usually a gradual one, with significant signs and subtle slips going virtually unnoticed in their magnitude.

We are often too consumed by living in the moment to think of the long-term implications and impact of events, practices, and pronouncements all around us.

We take in stride the civil and legal challenges of some of our defining institutions. As a result, a reference to God in our sacred creed is acceptable or dispensable contingent upon the prevailing political condition in which we find ourselves. Prayer in public schools was once acceptable. Now, it is not. Citing the Pledge of Allegiance in the classroom was once a given. Now, it is being challenged.

Other signs of moral decay are all around us and we tolerate them in the name of free expression.

In the name of musical expression, we tolerate and support the most vile lyrics where girls and women are debased, law enforcement officers are demonized, and sexual indulgence is encouraged and saturate our airways.

In the name of fashion, we tolerate the most indecent dress. It is a common occurrence to drive down the streets and see black, white, and Hispanic teenage boys barely able to walk because their pants are dragging half-way, or lower, on their behinds. Their underwear is often in view.

Many of our teen-age girls are often scantily clad with their navels showing, buttocks and breasts barely covered. If covered, some outfits are so form-fitting, they leave nothing to the imagination. Their make-up too often disguises and defies their age and innocence.

Such dress among our youth conjures thoughts of whether they or their parents understand the notion that clothes, and appearance speak volumes about who you are and what you are about.

The cry to clean-up or sensor the content of television programs and film seem to fall on deaf ears. While adult entertainment industry—the acceptable name for porn—is at an all-time economic high, it is readily accessible to our children. Anyone who is able to operate a remote control can have highly suggestive or explicit sex with just a click.

What have we gained from our willingness to be so tolerant of such destructive social behavior?

We have continual disintegration of the family unit, perpetual devaluation of and disrespect for human life as seen through the increase in violence, growing deterioration of our educational system across the board, and rampant civil disengagement.

What will it take for us to regain the courage to stand up for those moral truths that are so critical to the health of these United States? It is a strong sense of morality that guarantees freedom. It is the power of moral ideas that fuel, form and perpetuate our most sacred and civil institutions.

So, what can we do to address this decline in our own civility?

- As we gather with family members and friends, we can discuss those forces and conditions that are harmful to the family unit, and detrimental to a healthy community, identify what steps can be taken to stop them, and commit to taking one or more of those steps either as an individual or as part of a group.

• We must demand that our secondary and higher institutions of education recommit to a curriculum where learning about the political, religious and morals beliefs that formed this country is a requirement. Vigorous debate must take place about the dangers of a society that does not rigorously defend moral truths. Such debate need not be suppressed or feared.

Holding fast the principles upon which this country was founded, the common ideals that unite us, is a perquisite to securing our future.

We are what we believe.

Published November 29, 2003
The Kansas City Star

Being President Requires Honesty and Accountability

Being president requires honesty and accountability, in no small measure, in any kind of organization. Being president also requires a good measure of strength and humility. How can anyone be an effective president of anything without these personal qualities?

The gravity of the need of these traits to be present can be no greater than in the person who occupies The White House as President of the United States.

What about the need for institutional knowledge and respect? The President of the United States should always demonstrate a real command and understanding of the history of this country. He or she should show ultimate respect for the sacred principles, policies, and institutions on which this country was founded and on which its future depends.

Imagine what would happen to organizations, companies, governmental entities if the leader is allowed to consistently indulge in thoughtless, reckless, dishonest, and irresponsible behavior? Ultimately, those organizations, companies or governmental entities will not stand. Why do we think it will be any different for America? It is not.

The damage or ultimate demise may not be immediate nor permanent, depending on the age, experience and resilience of the entity that has fallen victim to someone who is not qualified. But, why on earth would caring and concerned individuals that stand to lose so much, be hurt, or seriously diminished by such leadership, allow it?

America is a strong, resilient, prosperous, and blessed nation when one considers and compares it to many other countries in the world. But even America cannot withstand the repeated undermining of principles, laws, and values that made it great in the first place.

All thinking Americans cannot afford to forget the fate of great nations in the annals of history. Remember Rome? That great unparalleled empire was not destroyed by external forces, but the weakness, discord, and corrupt practices from within. During the time of the Roman Empire, there was not a nation or enemy or earth that could have defeated or destroyed it. Romans allowed their great nation to be destroyed. Sounds familiar?

America is still the strongest nation on earth. But how long will it remain if caring citizens allow their leaders to continue to disregard sacred institutions, lie at will, show utter disregard for the principles on which this country was built, and dismantle the laws and policies that sustain it? Such behavior by a leader would not be tolerated anywhere else.

USING MY WORD POWER

Being president requires honest and accountability. Those are minimum requirements when it comes to being President of the United States.

Published November 7, 2020
https://janicesellis.com/blog

Billboards of President Barack Obama: Disrespectful and Downright Unpatriotic

It would be easy to say that the continual display of disrespect for President Barack Obama is the ultimate example that racism in this country is alive and well. No doubt, a case could be made that indeed the perpetrators and those who condone such acts are indeed racists.

What else can be concluded of the recent billboard in western Colorado that depicts President Barack Obama, in living color, as a terrorist, a gangster, a gay man and a Mexican bandit? This, in the wake of the billboard where the Tea Party portrays him as a socialist along with Adolf Hitler and Karl Marx, certainly begs the question.

And then will we ever forget the congressman from South Carolina who felt comfortable calling President Obama a liar out loud in a full house of Congress for all the country and world to hear and see. A historical show of disrespect for the man, but even worse for the Office of President and the Halls of Congress.

All of these acts are unprecedented. Did you see such displays during the presidency of Richard Nixon, Bill Clinton, or George W. Bush? Did you see billboards depicting their factual transgressions—Richard Nixon as a bandit complicit in the planning of the Watergate break-in, Bill Clinton in an uncompromising positions with a woman, or George Bush dancing on a bar in a drunken stupor?

Has President Barack Obama been a gangster, terrorist, a Mexican bandit? Oh, and a gay gangster, terrorist, and bandit at that?

Every real and respectful American should be screaming: ENOUGH, ENOUGH, ENOUGH.

Not to do so reflects badly on all of us. I hate to think what some of our global neighbors must be thinking.

Such blatant demagoguery and derogatory acts are the ultimate show of disrespect for the office of President of the United States of America. It is un-American. It reflects more negatively on the perpetrators and those who condone than it does on President Barack Obama.

Unfortunately, there are those who simply cannot get over the fact that America has a black man as president. They are either unwilling or incapable of extending President Barack Obama the benefit of the doubt that he is a qualified and able leader. Just as good, even better than many of his white predecessors.

History will be the ultimate judge of President Barack Obama. But history will judge our actions or the lack thereof as well.

Published October 19, 2010
USAonRace.com

Beyond September 11

A lasting victory against terrorism will be achieved only when we invest in educating ourselves and future generations on the peoples, cultures, religions, and lifestyles beyond our own.

Our nation can spend unlimited resources to find Osama Bin Laden, dead or alive, and behead Al Qaeda forever—perhaps. We can wage war to topple Saddam Hussein. Over time, we might even rid the "Axis of Evil" of its capability to spew wanton destruction on anybody or anything within its reach. But will winning these battles result in us winning the war on terrorism?

It begs the question, how can we ever hope to achieve a lasting victory if we, average American citizens, do not understand the enemy, all of its faces, and the fronts on which the war must be waged.

During the last year, we have been in almost a constant state of heightened alert, sometimes as a result of official warnings, but more often as a result of our own anxiety. Irrespective of its origin, our new role as watchdogs against becoming the victim of some camouflaged terrorist in our midst cannot be taken lightly. Watchdogs? Against what?

USING MY WORD POWER

A lone suicide bomber, a well-placed dirty bomb, an airborne germ against which we have not been immunized?

It may be true that the best offense against terrorism, in the long run, is a good local defense. But does that mean being a watchdog for irregular or errant behavior of someone who may or may not look or act like us?

During the last year, many new names, places, people, and things have crept into our sphere of consciousness, perhaps to reside there forever, as a result of newspaper articles and television news: Jihad, Koran, Al Qaida, Islam, Islamabad, Kabul, Taliban. But beyond the news, what steps have we taken to really gain a good understanding of what is threatening our shores, our way of life, and most importantly, why this might have happened?

September 11, 2001 will be earmarked in the history books as the day that changed America forever. It signaled to all Americans, irrespective of our race, ethnicity, religion, economic status, or dwelling place—urban, suburban, or rural—that we were equally disliked and disregarded in the eyes of terrorists who hate everything about our democratic way of life. We suddenly became one, united in our patriotic feelings and the desire to protect America and our way of life despite its imperfections.

Sometimes, it is amazing what it takes for different people from different walks of life living in proximity to each other to recognize the things we have in common—the things that bind us. To finally recognize that differences in skin color may not be the great divide we think it is. But, rather, other things like religion, economic disparity, a way of life often create and build the greatest chasms.

But with the events of September 11, we also have inherited an awesome burden. How do we achieve a lasting victory against terrorism? We must revisit, or bother to learn anew, and apply some critical lessons from history.

I am reminded of the memorable words of President Franklin Delano Roosevelt as the nation faced another crisis: "We have nothing to fear but fear itself." But I am also reminded of the age-old axiom that great civilizations are rarely destroyed from external forces, but rather from weaknesses from within.

What is notable about both pronouncements is that *ignorance* is often the common source of both fear and weakness. We cannot afford to remain in a bubble of ignorance, peppered with misplaced arrogance or blind pride. The ramifications for our future lifestyle and that of generations to follow are simply too great.

On a broader and lasting scale, terrorism will not be understood and defeated until we make a concerted effort to reduce the pervasive lack of knowledge among adults, and children alike, of emerging forces and ideologies that are harmful to our own.

It is both a local and national challenge.

Just last week, test results of high school students in Missouri reveal that most of our high school students are not meeting the minimum competency standards in the social, biological, and physical sciences. Missouri's student performance is not unique. How can we expect our children to become the physicists, chemists, social scientists, historians, astute ambassadors, and political leaders that it will take to wage and win wars of the 21st century?

Until we effectively address this major weakness in our armory, a lasting victory against terrorism will continue to elude us.

As we pause this Wednesday to remember and honor the ordinary citizens and heroes who lost their lives on that infamous September morning, we must also give serious thought on the ongoing obligation of those of us who were spared.

Published September 11, 2002
The Kansas City Star

Chipping Away of Protected Individual Rights

The chipping away of protected individual rights by the U.S. Justice department under the leadership of Attorney Jeff Sessions is virtually going unnoticed and uncovered by major media. Instead, the focus is on the Trump Administration's drama or latest revelation of the day. It makes for high viewership, maybe high ratings.

It is reminiscent of the legend that Rome burned while Nero played the lyre or flute, if indeed, he played anything at all. Legend has it that he played the fiddle or violin. But we know that is not true because neither existed during the first century. But really, whether folklore or truth, the point is well made. We tend to become occupied with frivolous and unimportant things at the detriment of more critical issues and priorities.

That seems to be the case because under the leadership of Attorney Jeff Sessions, there is a chipping away of protected individual rights. The Justice Department recently announced several measures that caring Americans should find concerning.

More states will be allowed to restrict voting rights, not only making it more difficult for blacks and the elderly to continue to vote, but also making it more difficult for first-time voters in traditionally disenfranchised groups. This is a gross chipping away of protected individual rights—one of the most basic. The right to vote.

More local police departments will again be able to operate without oversight, even though you can hardly go a week without hearing about aggressive police actions toward citizens who are not committing a crime. Often it involves young black males. More recently, policemen were overly aggressive with a white nurse in a hospital who was simply doing her job. Police brutality is still a problem in cities and towns all across America.

When prisons are overcrowded with young minorities men, primarily black men, who committed minor drug offenses, the Justice Department is pushing to have longer prison sentences for drug crimes. The Justice system that supposed to be blind discriminates against blacks and other minorities all the time. This, again, is an alarming chipping away of protected individual rights. Everyone is entitled to equal protections under the law.

Jeff Sessions is also preparing to challenge affirmative action measures that were put in place to create a level playing field for blacks and other minorities who were historically denied entry into colleges and universities to be able to be admitted. It has only been in the last forty to fifty years that blacks have been allowed to be admitted to colleges and universities.

There is a chipping away of protected individual rights, some of which were just recently gained when you look at the history of this country.

Does anyone care?

Published September 13, 2017
https://janicesellis/blog

The Church and the Clergy—A Moral, Social and Political Compass, Still

Some compare it with an anchor that steadies a fisherman's boat. Others may compare it to a lighthouse for the ship at sea that is trying to find its point of landing. Yet others see it as a compass to keep a community, a society, headed in the right direction or a beacon for those desolate souls who may have lost their way.

The Church. Still a viable and needed force in our daily lives, in so many areas, in so many ways. That became very evident in Kansas City when members of the clergy, with other community leaders, intervened to find a solution to the Dillard discrimination problem. It should be noted that the religious leaders kept their "hands to the plow" and their "eyes on the mark" until some resolution was achieved. And they are likely to remain faithful and keep the vigil until the promises are kept and change becomes reality.

Again, it was members of the Concerned Clergy in Kansas City who provided the leadership for the Faith-Based Village Meeting that took place at Penn Valley last

Saturday—the first of many village meetings to come. The primary goal of the Faith-Based Leadership Initiative is to research and develop recommendations and implement focused strategies for the formation of significant alliances designed to revitalize and strengthen the African American community of the inner-city of Kansas City. Members of the clergy appealed to professionals in the areas of health, education, and economic development to come together and begin a dialogue on the very areas that define the quality of life, or like thereof, for African-Americans in Kansas City.

The sessions on education, health and economic development were both enlightening and disturbing. For all who were present, the messages were clearly bugle calls. It was a rallying cry that the community cannot afford to stand by and not get involved in the areas of education, health services and economic development as they relate to the urban core. That if we truly expect to slow the forces of deterioration in these areas and begin the task of making things better, religious, and professional leaders much come together, take action, and keep a constant vigil. Not to do so is to allow the downward spiral to continue—our black children continuing to underachieve in chaotic, mal-focused, misdirected school environments; the poor and underemployed will still be unable to access quality health care services, receive the necessary health education to prevent diseases and maintain healthful living habits; and many of our elderly and indigent will be forced to continue to live in sub-standard housing, be forced to shop in price-gouging clothing stores, poorly-maintained grocery stores, paying sometimes twice as much for food, toiletries and other living necessities simply because of the neighborhood they live in. It was clear that no one should be content to sit back and not get seriously involved for there is so much to do.

We should not be surprised by this demonstration of leadership on the part of our ministers. Historically, many religious and church leaders have led the movements that resulted in political, economic, educational, and social change. We have only to think of St. Augustine, Martin Luther, Charlemange, St. Thomas Acquinas, and St. Francis of Assisi. To bring it closer home, we have had Adam Clayton Powell, Martin Luther King, Jr., Jessie Jackson, and countless others who have made a difference in their own communities, if not, indeed the nation.

Too often, church members and the ministers that lead them are our unsung heroes. So many spend great portions of their days, and nights, trying to make the lives of the neglected and downtrodden better. But when these leaders, take a greater step and move beyond the needs of their immediate congregations to address broader issues, it is a call for us all to line up with them, apply our time and talent to address community needs.

The church, the ministers—still calling us, as concerned citizens, as businessmen and women, as political leaders, as educators to do the right thing for fellow Kansas Citians.

It is up to us to heed the call.

Published June 25 – July 1, 1998
The Kansas City Globe

Confederate Statues and Memorabilia Belong in Museums

Confederate statues and memorabilia belong in museums and designated parks to remind all Americans of a period in this nation's history that was detrimental, inhumane, ugly, and which should never be repeated. It is enough to have lingering vestiges of racial conflict, inequality, and oppression prevalent today and still holding us back. There is no need to have statues to be in public places as stark reminders.

However, toppling, tearing down, and destroying statues and monuments, of those who were so pro slavery and led the charge to secede from the Union, is not the answer either. The resulting Civil War threatened the very existence of this country. What is the purpose of waving the confederate flag instead of or alongside the American flag? That flag along with confederate statues and memorabilia belong in museums and designated parks.

Removing those statues and monuments will not undo history. Such actions will not undo the horrible deeds of those men, nor the lasting destructive attitudes, laws, and practices that resulted from them.

But neither is displaying them, honoring them in public squares and other public spaces of southern cities, towns, and state capitals. They only serve to make a statement that this part of American history is laudable and something to be proud of. Sadly, many American who regale in those times and symbol will likely continue to do so in their hearts and minds. Confederate statues and memorabilia belong in museums and designated parks.

Much of American history is preserved in national and local museums where it is accessible to anyone who would like to revisit our past, visit it for the first time, or learn anew the real facts.

It is long past time that America's confederate history takes it rightful place within the walls of a national museum or several museums. Those reminders need not be destroyed. Future generations need to know the complete story of America's history—the good, the bad, along with a promising future.

It is healthy to acknowledge that any period of human enslavement, oppression, servitude, and persecution in a country's is, indeed, a shameful and inglorious one. It begs the question why would any decent, compassionate, ethical, if not God-fearing, person want to honor and revel in such a time with visible reminders. Confederate statues and memorabilia belong in museums and designated parks along with other relics of America's past.

The goal should not be to destroy history, but to learn from it. The outrage that we are witnessing in city streets and historical sites across America is a cry for us to learn from out past, and to begin to take meaningful and lasting actions to change it.

One united America—make the future America a special and better place for everyone.

Published June 23, 2020
https://janicesellis.com

Exercising the Basic Right to Vote

Exercising the basic right to vote is still a major issue in supposedly the greatest democracy on earth, the United States of America. Our history of extending this basic right to all Americans has, at best, been a spotty one. Perhaps, one of the main reasons is because originally, the United States Constitution did not define who was eligible to vote, leaving that decision to each state to determine.

It seems that exercising the basic right to vote in this great democracy has been problematic for one group or the other ever since. Voting, participating, and having our say in how we are governed, the essence of who we are as a country has been, and continues to be, seriously undermined.

One unintended, and some would argue intended, consequence has been getting government that *was not* of the people, for the people and by the people as we like to think and brag about. Well, maybe of, by and for a few.

At first, exercising the basic right to vote was extended only to white men who were property owners. Men and women who were not property owners could not vote in most states. Early in our history women could vote in a few northern states and jurisdictions if they owned property. Freed slaves and other non-whites could vote in a few jurisdictions if they met the property requirements.

But even the property requirement was eliminated for white men, and they were eligible to vote in all states prior to the Civil War, and of course, has continued to be so. But consistently denied to others.

Subsequent amendments to the Constitution prohibit any state from denying an American citizen the right to vote because of "race, color, or previous condition of servitude," the 15th Amendment that passed in 1870; or on "account of sex," the 19th Amendment passed in 1920.

We all know what those amendments have meant and haven't. Many states have and continue to institute policies to make it hard for certain citizens to vote, most notably, blacks, Native Americans, and other "undesirable" minorities. The measures being adopted in recent years, and even today, also target the elderly with unreasonable identification requirements.

First, many states required payment of poll taxes or reading standards, which many minorities could not meet. While that has been repealed, having various forms of identification when you get to the polls has taken its place.

Several states (Georgia, Texas, Kansas, Wisconsin, Indiana, Virginia, Tennessee, and Mississippi) have strict photo ID requirements to vote; other states simply require a Photo ID (Alabama, Florida, Hawaii, Idaho, Louisiana, Michigan, New Hampshire, Rhode Island, and South Dakota). The remaining thirty plus states have non-photo requirements that must be met.

Many of the states requiring photo IDs have not been shy about saying that the new requirements are there to limit those who can vote and to affect the level of turnout in the 2016 Congressional and Presidential elections.

It is 2016, and many citizens will find it difficult, if not impossible to vote in these very important elections because they cannot get the required ID. And those most affected will be minorities and the elderly.

And we wonder why the country and the political process are suspect and so divided. We are still fighting over exercising the basic right to vote. Is this an America that all Americans can believe in?

Published December 23, 2020
https://janicesellis.com/blog

Focus On the Values That Make America Great

During this divisive time in our nation, what would happen if we all paused to focus on the values that make America great? What would happen if we put our political, partisan, and selfish issues aside and focus on what is best for this country? We are at a critical crossroads. The very fabric of what defines America seems to be unraveling in front of our very eyes.

Even though America is far from perfect, there have been values that we, as citizens, have adhered to. We value individual rights. We value freedom of speech. We value representative government, where we expect those that we vote for to function in the best interests of ourselves, families, communities, and yes, our country! We value patriotism and love of country.

These are just a few of the values we honor and respect. There are many more outlined in our Bill of Rights, and the Constitution of the United States. During this very partisan and potentially destructive time in our nation's history, we need to take time to revisit and discuss these critical documents. We need to do so with our family, friends, and in community forums.

We need to focus on the values that make America great during a time when they seem minimized or forgotten. If we fail to do so, we may find ourselves vulnerable and carried on a path that will not be good for this country nor its citizens.

Most of us value honestly and integrity from elected officials and government employees just as we do from others that we interact with as we go about our daily lives. During these impeachment hearings, and the divisive, false, impartial information that surround them, out attention to truth and values are more important than ever. Listen critically. Focus intently.

Passive, intermittent attention on what is occurring is simply not enough.

Are the principles and practices that you value still being upheld by those in leadership positions at the local, regional, and national level of our governmental system? As difficult as it might appear, we cannot afford to turn a blind disinterest eye. There is too much at stake not to focus on the values that make America great. Especially now.

Not only is the quality of life as we know it at risk. How America will operate in the future is a stake. If you love America, as imperfect as it may be, promote and focus on the values that make America great.

Published November 18, 2019
https://janicesellis.com/blog

Another Fourth of July Holiday—Is It Just About Fireworks, Picnics, and Parades?

As we prepare to commemorate the last Independence Day celebration of this century, of the 2nd millennium, we should revisit the principles and privileges outlined in the Declaration of Independence and recommit ourselves to practice their fullest meaning in our daily lives. When we do not, we fail to take advantage of the opportunities that come with being an American, a Kansas Citian.

Pause a moment and ask, "What does the Fourth of July celebration mean to me?" When I look around and take inventory, "What does it mean in my city, my community?"

The Fourth of July celebration should be a time for each of us to take inventory of the political direction of our country, our city, our community. Are we making progress ideologically or have we abandoned our ideals? Are we moving forward, standing still, or losing ground? We need to not only ask some questions, but indeed answer them: Is America an environment of equal opportunity for all? Are all of its citizens afforded dignity, respect, equal access, equal treatment under all of the laws of the land?

Is there evidence in your community that the American dream is alive and well in Kansas City? If not, why not? And more importantly, what can be done to change it?

As we pause from work and gather with family and friends, perhaps discussing these questions could stimulate and inspire us to revisit the true meaning of the Constitution, the Bill of Rights and all of the amendments in between. Let meaningful dialogue punctuate—it doesn't need to replace, but rather just be a part of—the commercialism that usually competes for center stage.

Fireworks, T-shirts, and other memorabilia have their place. But the true meaning of the Independence Day is in need of careful examination and reflection.

Amid all the pomp, picnics, and fanfare, ponder for a moment what it means to be an American, an African American, a Hispanic American, an Asian American—whatever your racial and ethnic origin. You might examine whether you, as an individual, as a member of this melting pot, are truly *giving* and *living, ensuring*, and *enjoying, providing*, and *partaking* of all the opportunities this rich land affords?

If not, why not? Where does the responsibility, or the lack thereof, lie? What is your role in it all? We often feel that we cannot do anything or if we do, it will not make a difference anyway—an attitude we must change.

Could it be that too often we fail to exercise one of the greatest, most powerful rights we as Americans have—speaking up and speaking out?

USING MY WORD POWER

Speaking out still gets results. America, Kansas City or needed changes in your community did not come about through silence. Nor did needed changes occur as a result of complacency, apathy, or complaining without action. Whatever gains have been made at the national, state, or local level have often been as a result of many people being *willing* and *courageous* enough to speak out, and get involved, when it counted.

Yet, too many of us choose to remain silent about the things we see, the things we experience, the things we encounter. Our silence is often born out of fear of reprisal or feelings of frustration because we are not sure how or where we should make our observations known.

Imagine where America would be, or would there be an America, had George Washington, Thomas Jefferson, John Adams, Thomas Payne, decided not to speak out against religious persecution, taxation without representation? Imagine where African Americans would be in this country had it not been for Frederick Douglas, Harriet Tubman, Sojourner Truth, W.E.B. DuBois, Thurgood Marshall, Martin Luther King, Jr., and countless others who spoke out and risked their lives in order that the rest of us would have access to schools and higher institutions of learning, public accommodations, jobs. And what about the hundreds and thousands who spoke out, even lost their lives, to give African-Americans the right to vote? Imagine how many black elected officials we would not have.

There is a meaningful way to celebrate the Fourth of

July holiday weekend. Pause a bit and rededicate yourself to the great ideals and values upon which this nation was founded. There are important social, economic, and political issues all around that will impact you, your children, your children's children.

Speak out—loudly and clearly. Get involved for a better country, a better Kansas City, a better community. This generation and future generations need to hear our voices.

Published July 1 – July 7, 1999
The Kansas City Globe

Guns in the Hands of Babies

Where are we headed, America?

One first grader pulls out a 32-caliber handgun and shoots another first grader—all because of a spat on the playground the day before. We are talking about six- and seven-year-old children—one pulling out a gun and shooting the other one, dead.

If we think the incident was that simple. We are fooling ourselves.

We are still trying to understand the rash of teenagers going to school with semi-automatic handguns, rifles, bombs, and arsenals that would make the average drug dealer's house look unprotected by comparison, killing their fellow classmates, teachers or whoever got in their way.

And now we have someone hardly out of kindergarten picking up a gun and thinking that is the right solution to whatever is bothering him.

We understand that the child who did the shooting has not had a very positive or healthy living environment. His father is incarcerated. According to one officer's description of his living environment, it was akin to a flophouse—

lots of traffic, drugs, and different people. The gun he used was stolen. The people with whom he lived were irresponsible and left the gun in a place where the child was able to get it. And he had a history of troubled behavior in the neighborhood, according to his neighbors.

Perhaps, all of the above were contributing factors. Well, if that indeed is the case, as a society, we should be asking ourselves how many six and seven year old children—even younger—are at risk for being a victim or victimized by such conditions. If we are honest, much too many for us to become comfortable, turn our heads, and do nothing about it.

Both of those children are victims, the one who lost her life and the other who took it—victims of a society that fails too often to do more than spew out empty rhetoric, vacant promises, and too little resources to really address the problems.

It is ironic how we can find billions of dollars to fund space programs, housing, defense, and other projects of special interests. But there are so many young, helpless children at risk because we do not have adequate social service agencies and enforcement entities to identify them—let alone, intervene, and get them out of harm's way.

There is something definitely wrong with this picture.

Unfortunately, it takes a tragic incident like this to jar us out of our selective blindness—pretending we do not see or refusing to face up to what we see.

But how many other such incidents of a first grader shooting another—God forbid—will we have to hear about before we take notice and realize that we have some social cancers growing in our midst that we need to acknowledge and work to find lasting cures? Will it take a gun-toting 4-year-old kindergartner?

If we think the incident is not indicative of some deeper social problems that threaten the very fabric or our society, we are fooling ourselves.

Published May 15, 2014
https://janicesellis.com/blog

Illegal Drugs or Prescription Drugs

Illegal drugs or prescription drugs, the damage and destruction they can wreak on people's lives, and the lives of their loved ones, render the distinction between the two types of thieves meaningless.

Drug addiction, like cancer, has been and continues to be the plague of contemporary society.

But unlike cancer where there has been much progress in fighting its ravages and death sentences, the war against drugs cannot boast of a disease that seems to be in decline. Illegal drugs or prescription drugs, they are both taking their toll.

There was a time when it was almost expected that drug use was part of the entertainment world. People were not so surprised to learn that their favorite rock star, musician, or leading actor had some sort of addiction to alcohol or cocaine. While shocked or hurt at the news of an overdose that took some talented artist or actor, it still all seems a part of a world that did not touch us personally. That was then and so long ago.

Then there has been for a long time and continues to be the drug abuse that have plagued poor minority neighborhoods and ghettos for decades and across many generations. Way back when it was street drugs, like heroin, instead of designer elite drugs like cocaine that took its toll on the famous and not-so-famous, entertainers and regular joes alike.

Fast forward to today. When we have more knowledge about the damage of addiction, it seems to have had little effect on deterring usage. Much like smoking. While we know what first-hand and second-hand smoking can do to one's body and health and that of those nearby, innocent children notwithstanding, many people still smoke.

Today, the use and abuse of drugs is worse than ever. Heroin, cocaine, crack, methamphetamine use is at epidemic proportions in some parts of the country. But that is only part of the addiction problem. The use of prescription drugs, pain killers particularly, has its foothold as well. The illegal drug business boasts of being in the billions of dollars annually. What is the annual return on the sale of prescription drugs, which can be easily bought on the Internet as well as in the offices of unscrupulous doctors?

President Obama is asking Congress to increase funding for the treatment of addiction. That is part of the solution. We as parents, relatives, educators, and caring adults must begin early to show children, in stark terms, the risks in experimenting and using drugs. We must teach them to identify the signs of peers and the predatory practices of pushers.

And let them know that it does not matter whether it is illegal drugs or prescription drugs, the potential damage and destruction is the same.

Published December 8, 2019
https://janicesellis.com

In search of America's Voice

Where is America's voice? At critical points in the history of this country, it has, more often than not been resoundingly clear. But, today, it is garbled at best.

While one or more leaders may help define America's voice, clarify it, and epitomize it with their actions, the voice itself goes beyond a personality, the vocalization of precepts and principles or specific initiatives. Rather, its presence and power characterize ages, codifies eras, creates the culture, and more often than not, foretells the nature of a future society.

We have only to recall a few critical periods in America's history and the personalities that led us through them—from the Declaration of Independence to the end of the Cold War—to be poignantly, and sometimes painfully, reminded of the great void that exists today.

Where is America's voice? And if you are able to hear it, what is it saying? Are you clear about where we are headed domestically or globally?

Admittedly, there may not have always been agreement with the policies or way of life that came about as a result of a course America took, but, at least, historical accounts show that contemporaneous Americans had a better sense and understanding of the rallying cries, and the shared beliefs in which they were grounded.

Through the work and words of the founding fathers and the framers of the Constitution _ John Adams, Thomas Paine, George Washington, Thomas Jefferson, and others—America gained its voice and its course through the end of the eighteenth century was clear.

Throughout the nineteenth century, America's voice defined the ages from the establishment of institution of slavery to the Civil War that ended it. And the Jim Crow era that began after that war and lingered into the twentieth century until the Civil Rights Movement that fought to end it.

America's voice during these epoch-making times was represented by many. Abe Lincoln, Frederick Douglass, Strum Thurmond, Lester Maddox, George Wallace, Lyndon Johnson, Martin Luther King, Jr., to name a few.

In between, World War I was fought to make the world safe for democracy. Whether it did or not, it was followed by what has been dubbed as the Gilded Age where the rich got richer, the poor poorer. America roared in the twenties, crashed economically in the early thirties, and joined the world to defeat Hitler and Nazi Germany in the forties. And we lived and breathed the Cold War and its remnants for the next nearly fifty years.

We all know these seminal historical events and the leaders that brought us through them: Theodore and

Franklin Roosevelt, Harry Truman, Dwight Eisenhower, John Kennedy, Ronald Regan. During any of these periods, America's voice was discernible if not always strong. The times seem more definable, the voice clearer, even while we lived them.

A greater sense of American history and purpose was passed on from one generation to the next back then. It was inculcated in almost every aspect of our lives, from lively debate around the dinner table, the town square, to the classrooms. Today, well, there is the news and the internet.

Where is America's voice, today? Where are the political and philosophical giants that represent it?

With the current war on terrorism, it is easy to say that America's voice is still one that proclaims democracy and individual freedom as paramount at home and abroad. But that voice seems muffled by all the static and noise that has emerged around the reasons for the preemptive strike against Iraq. It seems further complicated with the news that Saddam is still alive, along with Osama. And American soldiers are still dying. A clear American clarion call still seems elusive.

Where is America's voice? What is it saying to us here at home? What is the message conveyed abroad?

America's voice is not just defined by politics. Lest we forget, the Gilded Age and the Great Depression are stark reminders. Where does the way we conduct business figure into the mix? The fact that we have so many corporate leaders who place a premium on individual wealth at the expense of the masses only promotes duplicity.

It is said that art and music reflect culture and culture reflects the values of a society. What do contemporary film, music and art say about America? Much of it, not very much.

How would you define this present age? Who are the leaders that will help America find its voice? It is not just left to the historians. We can shape it if we dare. Or we sit idly by and watch as we stumble into the future.

Published July 12, 2003
The Kansas City Star

Is America Still a Democratic Republic of the People?

When you see elected officials doing what lobbyists and big money contributors want them to do instead of what is in the best interest of the people who elected them, then it is a question that we need to ask. Is America still a Democratic Republic of the people?

Yes, there are the inalienable rights of life, liberty and the pursuit of happiness that are endowed to all American citizens. Yes, our form of government is participatory where the right to vote exists and can be exercised at every level of government, local, state, and federal. There are, what appears to be interminable, campaigns where we listen to the positions of candidates on issues that are important to the quality of our lives like education, healthcare, and taxes.

We vote for the candidate that seems to hold views and solutions similar to our own. Many of us even work to get elected the candidate who we perceive is the best. We truly believe that once he/she gets in office, he/she will propose policies and legislation that will represent our best interest, in the interest of the majority of Americans, and that of the country.

More often than not, and what seems to have become the prevalent practice, many elected officials, especially those in leadership positions, propose legislation and vote on policies that are in the best interest of the few—the rich, big business and their own selfish interest.

Often, these elected officials do something worse. They not only protect the interest of the few, but they do it at the expense of the majority, actually doing most citizens of this country more harm than good.

This is very evident by the recent actions of the U.S. Senate, and the U.S. House of Representatives when it comes to healthcare and tax reform. One must ask, is America still a Democratic Republic for the people?

Both houses of Congress seem determined to undo Obamacare (The Affordable Healthcare Act) in a way that will hurt millions of Americans rather than fix it and make it better. After repeated failure to repeal the Affordable Healthcare Act during the last seven years, both houses of Congress are still trying. The latest effort is attached to the proposed Tax Reform bill, which is suspect within itself.

In the proposed Tax Reform bill, President Trump and Republican Senators want to give corporations and the very rich tax cuts at the expense of the majority of ordinary citizens—even when many of the wealthy have told Congress not to cut their taxes. Many are saying they could even pay more taxes. Why give the rich a tax cut at all, and then cut healthcare provisions to pay for it?

This is not what most Americans want or voted for. Again, who are the elected officials representing? Is America still a Democratic Republic of the people?

Published November 16, 2017
https://janicesellis.com

How Much Does Racism Influence the Right to Vote?

A recent article, "Who Gets to Vote?" that appeared in *The New York Times*, addresses the pervasive practice of states denying Americans with criminal records the right to vote. The article noted that during the next Presidential election in November 2012, more than 5 million Americans will not be allowed to vote because of a criminal conviction in their past.

The problem is that this denial can remain in effect for decades or a lifetime. The article duly notes that the implications for this practice have a more devastating effect on the political power and influence of black communities all across the nation.

The article states, "Nationwide, 13 percent of black men have lost the right to vote, a rate that is seven times the national average." The article goes on to state, "But the ripple effects of large-scale incarceration does not extend well beyond the individuals who are imprisoned, and as a result minority communities throughout the country have lost political influence."

The negative impact is obvious, "It's a simple equation: communities with high incarceration rates have fewer votes to cast. The whole community suffers the result."

But this practice has an ugly history and is tied directly to race, racism and race relations and the seemingly unshakeable influence these negative forces have played and continue to play on the American political stage. The laws were purposefully adopted to counter the 13th, 14th, and 15th Constitutional Amendments, which ended slavery, provided equal citizenship to freed slaves, and prohibited racial discrimination in voting.

To make sure that the waterfront was covered, these laws were adopted following the Civil War and during the Reconstruction area along with laws that required literacy tests and poll taxes as barriers for blacks to be able to cast a vote. As if this wasn't enough insurance, the criminal disenfranchisement laws targeted those crimes for which blacks were more likely to be convicted such as theft, perjury, forgery—furtive offenses compared to the crimes committed by whites.

You might guess that southern states adopted criminal disenfranchisement laws more than northern states, but in those days some northern states joined the chorus, New York among them.

Fast forward to today. Of the 50 states, only 23 states have restored voting rights or eased the process to reclaim those rights if you have a criminal conviction. But it needs to be noted that even today some of the major states, that impact the outcome of a national election, have not only maintained these laws, but have gone so far as to roll back any reforms, the states of Florida and Iowa among them.

The other dynamic that is occurring today is the movement by many states to require a particular type of ID to be presented if one wishes to vote. It is known that the type of state ID being required will less likely be one that minorities, blacks, have.

What a catch-22. What a vicious cycle.

And if that is not enough, the very states that enforce the criminal disenfranchisement law which prevents anyone with a criminal record from voting (mostly black men), those same states count the prison population (again, mostly black men) to get their fair share of federal dollars for roads, bridges, Medicaid, and other dollars (entitlements and otherwise) every year.

What a deal! It is called "Getting them going and coming."

Voting. The very essence of this Republic. The path to individual empowerment in the political process and shaping public policy, the foundation of becoming a productive member of society. Why the persistent effort to suppress?

There continues to be efforts at the state and national level to restore the right to vote in federal elections to all American who have served and satisfied their prison sentence and who are trying to lead productive lives.

As a society, if we are about restoration, second chances to those who may have lost their way or many of whom may have been wrongfully imprisoned in the first place, should we continue to deny the basic sense of dignity and civic involvement?

What do you think?

Published January 31, 2015
USAonRace

Native American Nicknames and Mascots

How long will it take to admit and correct the injury and insult that is piled on by the continued use of Native American nicknames and mascots by high school, college, and professional sports?

Haven't we as a nation done enough to Native Americans? First, we came to this country pilfered, pillaged their villages, women, and children. We ultimately took the land and herded them off to reservations. They continue to be subjected to sub-standard education and poor health care.

As if this wanton and utterly disenfranchisement was not enough, we have continued to reduce their culture for our entertainment by using Native American nicknames and mascots – from the genre of western film (The Lone Ranger and beyond) to our national pastime of sports, baseball, and football most notably. Worse, we pass this on to our children.

Recently, the cry of "enough" has grown louder. The Smithsonian Museum of Native American History recently held a day-long symposium about whether the pro football team, the Washington Redskins, should consider changing their name and mascots. The mayor of Washington, D.C., sensitive to the issue has begun to use the "Washington Football Team" instead of the Washington Redskins.

During that day-long symposium, many attendants became sensitized to what Native Americans must feel when they see fans dressed as Indians and performing moves and dances that they haven't a clue of their sacred meaning. There were many converts during that symposium, many vowing never to wear war paint, don an Indian feathered headdress and mockingly perform an Indian dance, "the Tomahawk Chop," again. Such use of Native American nicknames and mascots show racial and ethnic insensitivity and ignorance of history.

A few weeks ago, the Michigan Department of Civil Rights filed a complaint with the U.S. Department of Education, requesting that all Michigan high schools be barred from using Indian nicknames and imagery as their school mascots.

An editorial appearing in a Michigan paper, The Holland Sentinel, says it well: "…White Americans who blithely adopt for their own entertainment images from a minority group, especially one as persecuted through history as Native Americans, are likely to offend that group. The portrayals are almost inevitably one-dimensional caricatures, perpetuating old stereotypes. Too many people who would never dream of wearing blackface or a serape and sombrero abandon their good judgment when it comes to Native Americans, reducing an entire culture to war paint and feathered headdresses. If you wouldn't flaunt these images on a reservation, then they're not appropriate in a Michigan high school either."

As a nation, a day-long symposium or a filed complaint, and other actions here and there are starts to take corrective actions. But they clearly are not enough.

The pervasive, persistent, and insensitive use of Native American Nicknames and Mascots in our most endeared sports at every level only reinforces the need for a public dialogue in communities across America.

Published February 25, 2013
USAonRace.com

Las Vegas Killing Spree Was Domestic Terrorism

The Las Vegas killing spree was domestic terrorism. So why aren't authorities and the media labeling it as such? The definition of terrorism, generally, is any calculated violence against innocent unsuspecting people by someone because of some political, religious, or ideological reason.

The definition of domestic terrorism is when such violence takes place in your own country against your own people.

While we may never know the political, religious, or ideological views of this mass murderer, we do know that he engaged in the worst act of violence against his fellow citizens in his own country.

We also know the killer was not an immigrant. He was not Muslim, black, or Hispanic. He was not a young man as some of the recent domestic terrorists have been. Based on what we have been able to learn so far, the killer was neither a recruit, nor sympathizer of ISIS.

While he does not fit the typical profile of a terrorist, he is still a terrorist. The Las Vegas killing spree was domestic terrorism, committed by a native born American. A white male who was beyond middle age, in fact a 64-year-old retiree, living in an upper middle class retirement community.

This terrorist was apparently relatively wealthy, owned property and was an avid and successful gambler. Prior to retirement, he was an accountant with a college degree and a U.S. government employee, working for the Postal Service and the Internal Revenue Service.

Why has this violent crime against innocent unsuspecting Americans not been labeled a terrorist act? The Las Vegas killing spree was domestic terrorism. The killer, an American born white retired male, considered normal so far, is a terrorist.

While authorities are trying to determine motive, find the answer to the nagging question, "Why?" they can at least acknowledge one thing: The Las Vegas killing spree was domestic terrorism.

No doubt, what is most fearful, and disconcerting is the apparent growing inability to profile a terrorist. What does a terrorist look like in America, today? The killer in the Las Vegas mass murders has destroyed the stereotypical profile.

How will America protect itself from the next domestic terrorist?

Published October 10, 2017
https://janicesellis.com

Moving Away From Great Principles That Built America

When you look at the current state of our country, are we moving away from great principles that built America? While far from perfect, America is still the greatest and most successful democratic republic in the world. But, when you look around, are we gaining or losing ground?

Our founding fathers, in forming the Declaration of Independence, Bill of Rights, and the Constitution, laid the foundation for greatness. They established this nation on the pillars of liberty, morality, law, and faith. But it appears, more and more, we are trying to weaken and ignore the very guideposts that have kept this nation moving in the right direction.

When the Constitution was first ratified in 1789, it was not perfect. It has been amended twenty-seven (27) times since its inception. What does that tell us? That we should continue to improve upon the great foundation of America. Instead, we appear to be moving away from great principles that built America. It is prevalent in the divisive, errant, and toxic public discourse.

The founders formed this country to exercise religious freedom. Yet religion seems to be interwoven in the political dialogue. Sadly, in a negative and divisive way. Faith played a very important role with the founding fathers in building this country. It was evident all around: in our currency, "In God We Trust;" in our Pledge of Allegiance; in our patriotic songs, in the public display of the Ten Commandments. Now religion is being used to divide and demonize.

As time has passed, faith has become entangled with the notion of religious freedom, and what has resulted is a kind of religious oppression—yes, using religion to oppress and divide, here in America. America is about freedom to worship. Faith is about believing in what we cannot see. Isn't that how dreams and greatness are realized? The founders had faith in God's provision for this nation. There is nothing in the Constitution that speaks to religion or denominational preferences.

Similar erosion is occurring in freedom of speech, of the press, and the right of assembly. If you pay careful attention to what is happening nationally, and in communities all across the country, you will see some alarming trends. Legitimate factual press, peaceful assembly, and protests, and civilized and factual speech are being demonized and vilified at every turn. This threatens the very existence of our democratic republic—the very existence. Yet, we seem not to be duly alarmed.

What must our founding fathers be thinking? Are we losing our way by moving away from the principles that built America, the foundational principles that made this nation great?

What is the environment, the national and local dialogue, telling you?

Published April 3, 2019
https://janicesellis.com

Nationalism Is Surging Amid Unprecedented Globalization

Communication technology and economic interdependence connect countries and continents more today than at any other time in the history of civilization. But nationalism is surging amid unprecedented globalization. Why?

No doubt if polls were taken, nationalism or one who proclaims to be a nationalist would mean different things to different people. But nationalism is generally understood to mean a country supports and puts its own interests above all else, often at the detriment or exclusion of other countries. A nationalist is one who strong identifies and promotes this practice.

Globalization is understood to mean the interconnectivity between countries and continents, primarily in terms of business and trade. Cultural knowledge and exchange, shared political interests, and policies have been byproducts, largely because of common well-being if not, indeed survival.

Global business and economic interests include the imports and exports of food, oil, cars, and other consumer goods, taking place between and among countries all across the world. Political interests and policies address issues like nuclear proliferation, global warming, and the fight against terrorism.

So, why in the last few year is a move toward nationalism increasing, and the voice of nationalists seem to grow louder. We see it growing among world leaders, America, and Britain in particular. President Trump has made the theme "America First" a central part of his platform and the executive actions he has taken during his tenure as president. More than one Prime Minister has made Brexit, the intense effort to remove Britain from the European Union, their priority.

Nationalism is surging amid unprecedented globalization. Why?

The proponents of nationalism, of putting the interests of their countries first, claims that the primary reasons are economic. But, it that the only reason? Where there has been a surge in nationalism and increase in those claiming to be nationalists, there has also been an increase in racial unrest.

There has been an increase in anti-immigration policies, closing of borders to refugees and those seeking a better way of life or political asylum. There has been an increase in violence against racial, ethnic, and religious groups who have been citizens for generations, some since founding of the country. This is particularly true in America and Britain.

Other less prominent countries are waging wars and ethnic cleansing, all under the umbrella of protecting national interests.

Nationalism is surging amid unprecedented globalization. Do the reasons why demand a closer look?

Published October 21, 2019
https://janicesellis.com

On September 11 Americans Became One

On September 11, 2001 Americans became one and the day will be earmarked in the history books as the day that changed America forever.

The shocking and horrific terrorist attack signaled to all Americans, irrespective of our race, ethnicity, religion, economic status, or dwelling place—urban, suburban, or rural—that we were equally disliked and disregarded in the eyes of terrorists who hate everything about our democratic way of life.

We suddenly became one, united in our patriotic feelings and the desire to protect America and our way of life despite its imperfections.

Sometimes, it is amazing what it takes for different people from different walks of life living in proximity to each other to recognize the things we have in common—the things that bind us. To finally recognize that differences in skin color may not be the great divide we think it is. But, rather, other things like religion, economic disparity, a way of life often create and build the greatest chasms.

But with the events of September 11, we also have inherited an awesome burden. We must revisit, or bother to learn anew, and apply some critical lessons from history.

I am reminded of the memorable words of President Franklin Delano Roosevelt as the nation faced another crisis. He boldly and confidently reminded the nation that "We have nothing to fear but fear itself." But I am also reminded of the age-old axiom that great civilizations are rarely destroyed from external forces, but rather from weaknesses from within.

What is notable about both pronouncements is that ignorance is often the common source of both fear and weakness. We cannot afford to remain in a bubble of ignorance, peppered with misplaced arrogance or blind pride. The ramifications for our future lifestyle and that of generations to follow are simply too great.

On a broader and lasting scale, terrorism will not be understood and defeated until we make a concerted effort to reduce the pervasive lack of knowledge among adults, and children alike, of emerging forces and ideologies that are harmful to our own.

It is both a local and national challenge that cut across race, ethnicity, age, gender, and socio-economic status.

As we pause this Thursday to remember and honor the ordinary citizens and heroes who lost their lives on that infamous September morning, we must also give serious thought on the ongoing obligation of those of us who were spared. All of us. Black, white, brown, yellow, alike.

Published September 11, 2014
https://janicesellis.com

Removal of Confederate Monuments

The removal of Confederate monuments will not get rid of the great racial divide that is on display all across America. Bigotry, racism, prejudices, disenfranchisement of groups of people based strictly on skin color and economic station in life will still be an ugly part of America.

The removal of Confederate monuments will not stop how blacks are perceived and treated in the workplace all over America.

The removal of Confederate monuments will not stop how blacks are treated by police and the criminal justice system; when blacks are stopped more often than whites with or without a legitimate reason; when once they are in the justice system, they receive longer and harsher sentences and judgements than whites for the same or lesser offenses. This is commonplace in towns and cities all across America.

The removal of Confederate monuments will not stop the perpetuation of the education achievement gap where black children are still locked in poor inferior schools; where black children who are in racially integrated schools are disciplined and expelled at much higher rates than white children for the same behavior and infractions.

The removal of Confederate monuments will not rid this country of the entrenched racism, economic and educational disparities that are the real problems. The Confederate Flag, monuments of generals that fought to maintain slavery and the southern way of life, committing acts of treason in the process, are just symptomatic of the racial problem that remains in America. Removing those symbols will only be a surface fix.

The removal of Confederate monuments will not erase the ugly history of America, and more importantly, the bane of evil that still remains as seen in the resurgence and boldness of white supremacy and blatant expressions of racial hatred.

Only facing this scourge, confronting it, and actively taking the necessary steps to make things better will have lasting meaning.

Sadly, even then, there will be those who will stay stuck in the false sense of racial superiority that is merely a relic of America's past.

Yes, Confederate flags and monuments are historical relics that too many are trying to preserve not because of their place in America's history, but in an attempt to determine America's future.

Published August 27, 2017
https://janicesellis.com

Role and Responsibility of the Press

Has the role and responsibility of the press changed? Instead of reporting the story factually and accurately, it seems that, more and more, the press is becoming a part of the story, often abdicating it role for the dramatic and ratings when it comes to the coverage of the 2016 Presidential Election. It is clearly evident in the coverage of Donald Trump and Hillary Clinton.

This is not the case with all of the press. But it is the case with too much of press coverage.

Who, which media, can the public rely on to be the objective observer, the reporter of the truth and facts, in deciding which of the candidates is most fit and qualified to lead this great nation and be the leader of the free world. Has the traditional role and responsibility of the press fallen victim to being a chaser of drama for ratings in contemporary society?

Our democracy has always faced the challenge of how it can work the best for the public good. This has become an even greater challenge during the last century, with the expansive and diverse changes in our nation's geographical and population growth. Our framers of the Constitution, even when the nation consisted of the original thirteen colonies, knew that the press had to play a critical and necessary role in providing and disseminating common and accurate information on which the public could come to some rationale conclusions, and best decisions.

Disseminating and communicating accurate information was important back then, and both even more important now. Furthermore, it has been clear during the history of the free press that there needs to be a clear distinction between accurately reporting facts and events and expressing or pushing an opinion about those same facts and events. While both may be necessary, both must also be based on verifiable truths to be valuable and honorable.

But when you look at much of the press coverage of the 2016 Presidential Election, the lines between presenting and vetting the facts versus putting forth an opinion are at a minimum very blurred. More often than not, facts, opinions, misrepresentations, propaganda, and downright demagoguery have become so mixed that truth came seem hard to find. What the public ends up getting is a representation, a distorted picture, parading as truth, and that is downright dangerous.

There is some fact checking by some members of the media, but not nearly enough by some reporters and pundits alike. And yet the public is supposed to get behind the best candidate that will be in the best interest of individuals, families, and our nation. What is the role and responsibility of the press in making sure that the public is getting the best and most accurate information on which to make that choice?

What is a concerned, and likely confused, public to do in the weeks ahead? First, we need to be vigilant by relying on multiple sources for our news. We must take the time to consult print, TV cable news outlets, radio, and social media. We must critically assess and compare the sources of information and sort the facts from opinion and downright misrepresentation.

When it comes to Hillary Clinton and Donald Trump, listening and hearing what is coming from "the horses' mouths" is more critical than ever. If you rely solely of the reportage or lack thereof, sadly, you may be getting a much-distorted picture of what the truth really is when it comes to what they have actually said or done.

The role and responsibility of the press, as the disseminator of facts and truth, is needed more than ever.

Will reporters and pundits, alike, please stand up.

Published September 10, 2016
https://janicesellis.com

Selection of Kamala Harris Moves America Forward

As the first black woman candidate for Vice President, the selection or Kamala Harris moves America forward in so many ways. This is a historical moment, pregnant with major opportunities for this nation to let go of its oppressive, and discriminatory past when it comes to race and gender.

Amid the excitement among people of color, women, and everyone who truly see race and gender as positives and assets rather than negatives and liabilities, the selection of Harris is an important milestone in this country's history. That will be the case whether the Biden-Harris ticket succeed in winning the race to lead America or not.

The selection of Kamala Harris moves America forward in so many ways. First, in addition to her qualifications and experiences as an election officials, she represents what America is all about. America was built my immigrants. Harris is the daughter of immigrants. Her mother immigrated from India, and her father from Jamaica. They both contributed to American life in their respective professional fields. As a descendant of immigrant parents of color, Kamala Harris is a great example of what America is all about.

Secondly, the selection of Kamala Harris moves America forward when it comes to the centuries of struggle of women, especially black women. Black women have had a unique struggle in this country in so many ways, beginning with being denied basic respect, a sense of self-worth, and dignity as members of American society. Black women continue to be marginalized when it comes to equal employment, equal pay, and career opportunities. Black women have lived in double jeopardy simply because of being black, and a woman.

Thirdly, Kamala Harris is a grand example of what women, black and white, can achieve in this country. She will be an inspiration to girls all across America, irrespective of their skin color, their ethnicity or racial identity. They will see that they can achieve no matter where their parents came from, or their station in life. Girls all across America will know that they can break the bonds of oppression and inequality—whatever forces try to hold them back.

What a transcendent time in this nation's historical journey. The selection of Kamala Harris moves America forward in so many ways, spoken and unspoken. Each eligible voter will have to honestly assess whether they are willing to evaluate her worthiness and qualifications to be Vice President, potentially President of the United States of America, irrespective of her race and gender.

The looming question: In the coming weeks, if it proves that the Biden-Harris ticket is best to lead America during these challenging times, will the destructive vestiges of racism and sexism continue to hold America back from voting to move forward, from making the best effort to overcome its current struggles, from putting her in the best positions to achieve greatness?

At this time in history, each voter has a major decision to make, which could determine the course of America's future...

Published August 12, 2020
https://janicesellis.com

Shaping Public Opinion Is An Awesome Responsibility

Whether via television, radio, newspapers, or the Internet, the business of shaping public opinion is an awesome responsibility that should never be taken lightly. There is just too much at stake when you live in a democratic republic like the United States of America.

Yet, it has become big business. So many voices engage in it every day, as their major profession, under the guise of being an authority, an expert, or someone "in the know." Unfortunately, millions of unsuspecting Americans not only believe in them, but count on them for accurate information and direction.

These are Americans who for whatever reasons do not have access to necessary information or lack the access or time to find out the facts for themselves. So, they go to other sources, on their favorite TV/Cable News station, radio personality, Facebook, and Twitter connections. Too often, many of these personalities are pushing partisan positions, political agendas, distorted or down-right fake news and falsities.

Yet the unsuspecting public often cannot discern fact from fiction. Shaping public opinion is an awesome responsibility and if you are not about promoting truth and facts that will lead to the good and well-being of your audience, indeed society, you should not be about it.

Manipulating the public on distorted and false information is not only an injustice to the public that is attending, but also to others when actions or inactions are based on the lies and distorted information. Lies and fake news have a ripple effect. It is seen every day in the misplaced inaccurate information saturating cable news, radio and TV talk shows and social media.

Shaping public opinion is an awesome responsibility and should be grounded in a purpose that is designed to promote the best good for the greatest number. It should consist of presenting the facts and truth. It should be in the public's best interest and not to advance some selfish interest, or the welfare of a group, or the powerful few.

It is false, distorted, fake information and news that breed extremists, racists, bigots, terrorists, and all manner of scoundrels—the dregs of society, who takes advantage of social and individual progress. Too often, such extremism results in harm, even death.

We all can be about shaping public opinion within our orbit of influence, from family to colleagues, community, city, state, and nation. We only need to be clear of our purpose in doing so.

USING MY WORD POWER

Shaping public opinion is an awesome responsibility, no matter who we are trying to influence or be influenced by.

Published February 6, 2020
https://janicesellis.com

Terrorism Beyond and Within Our Borders

Terrorism beyond and within our borders, how will we successfully win this war? Or will it become a part of our way of life, to be watchful, even fearful of those who look or do not look like us if they act suspicious or look out of place?

The terrorist attack in Brussels, Belgium is another painful reminder of the times of which we live. ISIS is claiming responsibility. But ISIS is only part of the problem when it comes to terrorism.

Are we approaching or have we entered the Age of Terrorism? We have lived through two world wars, the Cold War, and the Nuclear Arms Race on a global level. There have been many regional wars where the United States has been engaged at one level or the other: The Korean War, the Vietnam War, and more recently the wars in Iraq and Afghanistan.

And now, there is the war against terrorism, only this enemy is more amorphous, not neatly defined or contained, philosophically or geographically. The enemy could be seas and continents away or they could be in your country, your city, your neighborhood. Terrorism beyond and within our borders, sadly is becoming a way of life.

USING MY WORD POWER

While the typical terrorist has been thought to have Middle Eastern origins (from Iraq, Iran, Yemen, Saudi Arabia), that only represents one profile. While it may not be the norm, a terrorist could be anyone from any ethnic or geographic region. In recent months we have seen American, African, Asians and Europeans, white and black become radicalized and sympathetic to the terrorist cause.

So where is the enemy? The reality is the enemy could be anywhere. That is not to engender fear or hopelessness in terms of being able to enjoy the safety and security that has defined America for centuries. Except for the Civil War, and the terrorist attack of 911, America unlike most other countries in the civilized world has been spared the ravages of war in its homeland.

But is our sense of safety, of being all powerful and untouchable, a thing of the past, an era that has slipped in the pages of history as part of the golden age of an American fortress? For we, like the rest of the world, have become vulnerable to an enemy that places little or no value on life, including their own. Terrorism beyond and within our borders can strike at any time.

Our intelligence capability, our military might, and our police protection provide a great element of comfort. But it will take us all to thwart, minimize and defeat this enemy. We must educate ourselves about the many facets and faces of terrorism. We must educate our children in way that will help them better understand and manage, without paralyzing fear, the world.

Knowledge and vigilance will be the average citizen's greatest weapon to minimize being a casualty of this war – terrorism beyond and within our borders – that likely will not be defeated anytime soon.

Published March 22, 2016
https://janicesellis.com

The Influence of Religion in American Politics and Public Policy

Whenever it is convenient or serves some political purpose, we are reminded that "separation of church and state" is an important aspect of our Republic. But is it? Has it ever been?

There are those who would like to believe it, advocate it, and even act upon the notion. But a close look at the history of this country shows that God and religion have always been presence and promulgated.

God and religion were an integral parts of colonial life and remains so in the 21st Century. Fundamental to the lasting association of religion and state is that our founding fathers were seeking freedom from religious oppression. God is reference in our country's most sacred documents, from the Declaration of Independence to our Pledge of Allegiance. A reference to God is imprinted on our currency and in the verses of some of our most patriotic songs.

Religion or the church, in the eyes of most Americans, is still deemed a viable and needed force in our daily lives, in so many areas, in so many ways.

Has there ever been an election in recent history where religion, "the church," has not wielded influence? Whether it is the evangelical Christians, the religious right, the Vatican, or some other faith-based group, the influence of religion cannot be denied. And such influence could not be more evident than in issues such as abortion and same-gender relationships. Those two issues alone seem to influence the actions of religious groups on the public or political stage more than any other—more than the scourge of war, hunger, and other human conditions.

While at some level in the public policy arena, the separation of church and state is a positive and productive position, so is the strategic alliance and partnership. The "Faith-Based Leadership Initiative" that began during the George W. Bush administration recognized the value in eliciting such a credible community institution to address some of the most pressing community issues, particularly in poor minority communities across the country.

The primary goal of the Faith-Based Leadership Initiative is to research and develop recommendations and implement focused strategies for the formation of significant alliances designed to revitalize and strengthen ethnic communities in blighted and economically-depressed urban areas. Members of the clergy appeal to professionals in the areas of health, education, and economic development to come together and begin a dialogue on the very areas that define the quality of life.

In addition to the founding fathers, historically, many religious and church leaders have led the movements that resulted in political, economic, educational, and social change. We have only to think of St. Augustine, Martin Luther, Charlemagne, St. Thomas Aquinas, and St. Francis of Assisi. To bring it closer home, we have had Adam Clayton Powell, Martin Luther King, Jr., Jessie Jackson, and countless others who have made a difference in their own communities, if not, indeed the nation.

Wailing against abortions, gay marriage should not be what defines the influence and impact of religion and the church in the contemporary public policy arena. The church, its leaders, and members, is doing much more to shape, influence and enact public policy. So many spend great portions of their days, and nights, trying to make the lives of the neglected and downtrodden better—efforts to improve housing, reduce crime, spur economic development.

Separation of church and state? Why not forge a stronger alliance to tackle those stubborn problems that plague communities all across this nation, whether in the area of quality educational achievement, reduction in blight and crime, and stimulus for much-needed economic development?

The influence of the church is ever present, why not take advantage of its fullest potential?

Published November 8, 2011
USAonRace.com

Who Are We America: Who Are We Becoming?

This is the first of a series of articles about the identity crisis confronting America here at home and on the world stage.

Who are we, America? Who are we becoming? If those are not questions many of us have asked ourselves, audibly, during and since the election, it is difficult to imagine that these questions have not crossed our minds. Whatever one might think about the things that were said and done during the 2016 Presidential primary and general election campaigns—whether you approve or disapprove—there are real reasons to be concerned about America's collective identity.

Do we still have a collective, unified, identity as a nation? There are some who may think we never have had a real sense of oneness, that that proverbial melting pot has only existed in a fantasy of what many of us have simple hoped that America is or would come to be.

Melting pot? Is that the impression you had during this election with such open unabashed and unashamed expressions and vitriol toward entire groups of people who did not look like us, worship like us, dress like us, but who were no less Americans? Groups of people who have not only help build and made America what it is but who continually help to sustain and keep America.

Who are we, America? Who are we becoming?

During this election, what happened to the cherished and prized notion that America is great because it is a melting pot? What happened to that great phrase from Emma Lazarus's sonnet, New Colossus, "Give me your tired, your poor, your huddled masses…" that has become such a mantra in American history? The plaque at the base of the Statue of Liberty reads: "Give me your tired, your poor, your huddled masses yearning to breathe free, the wretched refuse of your teeming shore. Send these, the homeless, tempest-tossed to me, I lift my lamp beside the golden door!"

Lazarus wrote the poem to be auctioned off at a fundraiser to finance the pedestal upon which the Statue of Liberty sits. The poem had been forgotten until the plaque was placed at the base of the statute. The only inscription on the Statue of Liberty itself is on the tablet in her left hand, which says JULY IV MDCCLXXVI (July 4, 1776), the day the United States adopted the Declaration of Independence.

Whether we reflect on the plaque or the inscription of that great national symbol of liberty, what does it really mean? What has it come to mean?

Who are we, America? Who are we becoming? Those are questions which should concern us all.

Published December 2, 2016
https://janicesellis.com

The Popular Vote and the Electoral College

This is the second of a series of articles about the identity crisis confronting America here at home and on the world stage.

The popular vote and the Electoral College provide a good example of the identity crisis confronting America. It begs the question how many of us truly understand how or why a candidate that does not win the majority of votes cast can indeed become the President of the United States. Why should winning the most electoral votes decide instead?

The framers of the Constitution did their best to put in place a measure that they thought would insure the fairness and integrity of equal representation among voters in this most important decision. That the selection of the President could not be determined solely by the largest states with the largest populations, leaving voters in small or middle-size states at a disadvantage.

The final decision of who becomes President is based upon the vote by the 538 electors, or members of the Electoral College, who represent the districts of the House of Representative the Senate and the District of Columbia. Who are the 538 electors? Each state gets one vote for each of their House and Senate representatives, which would be a total of 535 (435 members of the House and 100 for the Senate). The District of Columbia has 3 electors.

While the process might seem crystal clear, it really is not easily understood by many voters. No matter how many popular votes a candidate might get, they must also win 270 of the United States Congressional districts (representing those in the House and Senate) to become President. Donald Trump won most of the Congressional districts, 306 of them while Hillary Clinton won 2.86 million more actual voters, the popular vote.

On Monday, the 538 members of the Electoral College will officially cast a vote for President, the results of which will not be known until January 6, 2017.

But, in the meantime, there are many who would like to revisit the role of the popular vote and the Electoral College in determining who ultimately becomes president of the United States. There continues to be misunderstanding, misleading information and beliefs among concerned citizens. Over 52% of Republicans believe Donald Trump won the popular vote. More and more Democrats believe that Russia and FBI Director James Comey cost Hillary Clinton to lose key states. This only adds to undermining an electoral process that has worked for centuries.

Do you think the electoral process that we have used for the last 227 years should be changed? Can it no longer protect the democratic process we hold dear in America? The popular vote and the Electoral College. Can they not remain a pillar that is so much a part of America's identity as a strong Republic whose democratic process still stands out as the most honest and transparent in the world?

The popular vote and the Electoral College. They need not further divide America when they have worked so well together. They both are critical components of our, and America's, identity as a nation.

Published December 18, 2016
https://janicesellis.com

Should the President Be America's Role Model

This is the third of a series of articles about the identity crisis confronting America here at home and on the world stage.

As we approach the inauguration of the 45th President of the United States, should the President be America's number one role model? It is a question not only worth asking, but one in which we need to all answer, if only within ourselves.

One would like to believe that few rationale people would deny that the President should be America's role model. First as the number one citizen, but also as a decent, ethical, moral, caring and just human being. The person who occupies the office should be the best representation for all Americans.

Should the President be America's role model? What do you think?

Some of our past presidents have been better role models than others. No doubt, we all can point to ones who have been good examples and others who not only let themselves down, but family, citizens, the nation, friends, and allies around the world.

So where are we today, my fellow Americans? Where do we stand when it comes to the notion that we have always expected our President to be America's greatest example of a citizen, consistently demonstrating decency, respect, class, and decorum?

Whether we agree with the President's position on every policy or not, we should never have to question or be ashamed of how he conducts himself or how he speaks to and about others. Reason, rationality, decency, respect and being informed should guide his every utterance, every action. Should we expect facts and honesty to be important and a part of the reputation of our President, the Leader of the Free world?

America is at a critical crossroads when it comes to its identity—not only to its citizens and their children, but to the world and the world's children.

Should the President be America's role model—the consummate example of what America stands for? Should he, by his speech and actions, always confirm America's Constitution, its creed, and its character?

As we approach the inauguration of the nation's 45th President, we must ask the question: Does America's chief identity no longer reside in its Commander-in-Chief, in its most powerful and visible citizen? The President?

If so, America, where are we?

Published January 15, 2017
https://janicesellis.com

The World Is Watching the United States Senate

During the impeachment trial of President Donald J. Trump, the world is watching the United States Senate in how they carry out their sworn duties under the U.S. Constitution. Not only will the world be watching, but so will the nation, its voters, its voting citizens, and its children.

What messages will members of the U.S. Senate send to the many who are counting on their sense of duty, their sense of honor, their sense of patriotism? Will they each honesty seek the truth and facts, as they attempt to arrive at the right verdict? Will they each be able to set aside bickering and political partisanship to do the right thing for America?

Will each Senator be beholding first to the Constitution, to which they swore a solemn oath to always do the lawful and right thing to protect and promote the well-being of the United States of America? Will they bother to find out the wishes of the voters who put them in office? More importantly, if those voters are misinformed will the Senators bother to informed them with the facts?

The world is watching the United States Senate in how they conduct this trial. But, not only the world, but voting citizens, and impressionable young people who may want to enter into public service. What about all the children who model the behavior they see in adults? How will they come to value the meaning of taking an oath, seeking the truth, and acting on facts, putting the interest of others before their own?

Our allies across the world and other fledgling democracies have an interest in this trial and its outcome.

But there is a lot riding on this trial, other than the outcome. How it is conducted will be just as, if not, more important. For if the trial is carried out correctly, the world, the nation and other impressionable minds watching will be the better for it. No matter what the outcome, it will be more acceptable if a fair and real trial has occurred rather than a partisan side show.

As the trial unfolds, it will become clear whether partisan politics will trump the U.S Constitution, the rule of law, and the values America holds dear. It will become clear whether lies will trump truth. It will become clear whether misinformation will trump facts. It will become clear whether each Senator puts their own selfish interests ahead of what is in the best interest of the country, its citizens, and their constituents.

As the impeachment trial of President Donald J. Trump unfolds, the world is watching the United States Senate, along with the nation, its young people, and its children.

America's future is at stake, as history will surely judge. Hopefully, not harshly. The senators are obligated to vote for the current and future well-being of America.

Published January 15, 2020
https://janicesellis.com

Time to Redefine Domestic Terrorism Regardless of the Motive

Whether it is madness born of mental illness or an extreme religious or political ideology, it is time to redefine domestic terrorism regardless of the motive. More importantly, steps must be taken to prevent it from occurring. If the perpetrator did not have easy access to high-powered military style guns, the two incidents of mass murders of the magnitude that we have seen in the last month would not have occurred. Period.

It is time, past time, to implement better gun control policies in a country that boast of being among the most civilized in the world. And, boasting is all it is since we lead the world in gun ownership, and incidents of mass murders. There are valid studies that confirm that the primary reason the United States has among the highest incidents of gun violence is because of the number of guns in circulation.

It is time to redefine domestic terrorism regardless of the motive. It is domestic terrorism when a madman or madwoman randomly kills innocent people in a public venue whether he/she has extreme religious, political, ideological views, or is suffering from mental illness.

If you take a semi-automatic or rigged automatic gun and walk into a church, a bar, a shopping mall, a crowded theatre, or set up a tripod in a hotel window as a sniper and begin rapidly firing that gun, killing unsuspecting innocent children and anyone within sight, it is domestic terrorism.

It is terrorism that happens because such "apparently" random acts wreak havoc, death, and destruction on innocent people, their families, their communities, and the entire nation. It is time to redefine domestic terrorism regardless of the motive. Such acts of terror are a direct threat and infringement on the inalienable rights of life, liberty and the pursuit of happiness afforded all citizens. Just think about it.

What is the difference if such heinous acts are committed or inspired by a member of some extreme group, a lone wolf, or deranged person? In many ways, they all suffer from mental illness. The senseless carnage, the wanton loss of innocent lives, is the same.

Most of these incidents are well thought out and planned regardless of the state of mind of the shooters. It appears there is sanity amid the madness.

It is time to redefine domestic terrorism regardless of the motive before it becomes, and is accepted as, a normal part of life in America, resulting in those inalienable rights of life, liberty and the pursuit of happiness being severely diminished.

Published July 8, 2017
https://janicesellis.com

Two Americas Masquerading As One

There has always been two Americas masquerading as one. The election of Donald Trump as president has brought one front and center. Some may think that is a negative, bad thing. But is it?.

It cannot be ignored that more than sixty-million Americans voted for Donald Trump. They voted for him apparently because he promised to do what they wanted him to do. They voted for him because he apparently expressed views that they agreed with—whether about women, minorities, the environment, or the economy.

There has always been two Americas masquerading as one. It must also not be ignored that over sixty million Americans voted for Hillary Clinton—almost three million more than did for Donald Trump.

What does it all mean?

It means that those who claim to be citizens of one America are tolerant, embracing, and believe in the equality of humanity, regardless of skin color, regardless of a person's station in life, regardless of where a person lives. Citizens of this America honor and believe in the principles, rights and privileges outlined in and guaranteed by the Constitution.

Citizens of the other America is more tolerant, more discriminating and believe that America belongs to only them, again based solely on the color of their skin. They are willing to deny, to forget, and to ignore the Native Americans who were here before their ancestors arrived. Citizens of this America choose to ignore and to forget that this country was built on the backs of black slaves and other immigrants whose skin color came in different hues and shades.

There has always been two Americas masquerading as one, but both fighting for influence, fighting for dominance when it comes to politics, economic stability, and educational achievement. Both, under one flag proudly representing, tugging, and diametrically opposed forces—both claiming to be the right path toward greatness.

There are two Americas. There has always been two Americas masquerading as one great benevolent melting pot.

What a journey! One America seemed to have been winning until recently.

Which America are you a part of?

Which America do you claim as yours?

More importantly, which America will prevail?

Maybe neither because there are those who are determined to move America forward by going backward. And there are those equally determined not to allow them. Which America will prevail? Maybe neither.

Published August 30, 2017
https://janicesellis.com

U.S. Treasury Confronts Race and Gender

The U.S. Treasury department confronts race and gender issues in the recent announcement of the changes to occur on our paper currency. The most noted is the impending changes on the $20 bill. Harriet Tubman will appear on the front of the new $20 bill that will be unveiled in the year 2020.

Other paper currency will also get makeovers. The $5 and $10 bills will be redesigned to include suffragist leaders and civil rights scenes, including adding images of Eleanor Roosevelt, Marian Anderson and Martin Luther King, Jr to the back of the $5 bill. Portraits of five suffragist leaders and women's suffrage march will be on the back of the $10 bill.

Once these changes occur, it will be the first time in American history that an African American will be on a major and common medium of exchange. There are billions of $20 bills in circulation. It has been more than a 100 years since a woman was featured. This will also be a first when the changes occur on the back of the $5 and $10 bills.

While the announcements were just made, social media is abuzz with positive and negative comments about the changes, bringing the issues of race and gender again to the forefront. Many approve of the change of putting Harriet Tubman of the front of the $20 bill and moving Andrew Jackson to the back of the bill. Many do not.

While the noise will abate in the coming days, it is sure to re-ignite when the new paper currency is released. Boldly, the U.S. Treasury confronts race and gender issues in this country in making these proposed changes to our most commonly used paper currency.

Hopefully, this will help rid contemporary society of the need to hold on to the negative divides of race and gender.

Who knows? By the time the bills hit the streets many issues of race and gender will have also become a part of the history books and less in our everyday lives.

Published April 21, 2016
https://janicesellis.com

Values and Laws That Make America Great

The values and laws that make America great are at risk for being replaced by ones that are less noble, less honorable, and less workable. Where are the defenders of the Constitution and its Amendments that have set this nation apart from any other? What has happened to respect for and adherence to the rule of law? What has happened to freedom of the press? For starters. This erosion, like cancer, is spreading.

Fundamentally, it seems our representative government, which should be *of* the people and *by* the people is losing its way. The voices and defenders of truth and honesty, when it comes to public discourse and advancing public policy, seem to be drowning in a sea of lies and distortions. The lies and distortions are coming from those who hold the most visible and powerful positions in this nation: The President, some Senators, and some Representatives.

Are we really becoming a country, a citizenry that finds acceptable the blatant disregard for honesty, truth, and the rule of law? Is such behavior the new normal? The values and laws that make America great are being ignored and turned upside down. To whom do we turn?

America, the beautiful. Is it now only a song, with empty words? No doubt, many of us long to hold on to what makes America beautiful. No doubt, many of us long for conduct and decorum from our leaders that will honor America and its citizens. No doubt, we long for a President, Vice President, Senators, and Representatives who are great role models.

There was a time when aspiring to be a public servant, an elected official, was an honorable and noteworthy profession. Who can you point to as great role models for your children, your grandchildren, for yourself? Who do you look up to as a model public official, who works for the best interest of the people who elected him/her, who works for the best interest of America?

What we are witnessing today from the highest offices in our land is not just shameful, hurtful, it is putting the very values and laws that make America great at risk.

The future of America and how it will be governed is at a critical crossroads. We, the people, can only determine which road will be taken.

Published September 27, 2019
https://janicesellis.com

Violence—As American As Apple Pie?

Could this week be more than just a time to remember?

Whether we care to or not, we will be forced to remember some of the worst acts of wanton violence that have occurred on American soil during this week of April, all within the last decade.

First, there was the Waco tragedy where more than 80 men, women and children lost their lives in a flurry of bullets and a blaze of flames. Both sides, the FBI, and the religious sect of the Branch Davidians, fervently believed that they each were exercising their rights as outlined in our Constitution.

Then two years after that tragedy, in this same week in April, we had the bombing of the federal building in Oklahoma. More than 160 unsuspecting men, women and children lost their lives because some crazed former US marine thought it fitting justice to take an arbitrary number of innocent lives as retaliation for those lost at Waco. In some warped and sick notion, Timothy McVeigh and his cohorts thought they were upholding some revolutionary American principle in the American way.

And this week in April, a year ago, two teenage boys feeling alienated, disenfranchised, unaccepted in a well-to-do suburban community in Colorado plotted to kill all of their schoolmates and teachers. They succeeded in taking thirteen lives before they took their own.

These extraordinary acts, like bugle calls and blaring sirens, made us pause, take notice perhaps for a spell. But what about the litany of warning signs: The other school shootings that occurred not that long ago in Pearl, Mississippi, Paducah, Kentucky, Jonesboro, Arkansas _ all before those in Columbine Colorado. Fortunately, this past March, similar plots in Chimacum, Washington and West Palm Beach, Florida were discovered in time to prevent another senseless loss of life.

As we reflect on these catastrophic events, could it possibly be a turning point for us to seriously do something about the consequences our tolerance and glorification of violence has wrought?

Violence and our penchant for it are all around us. We seem to glorify violence _ from the acts of war, real and deified in film, from professional sports to recreational sports in real games and video games.

Has this appetite and indulgence of violence gone too far? Are the effects slowly coming home to roost in ways that we did not imagine?

A few weeks ago, the nation was stunned by a six-year-old first grader taking a gun to school and killing another because of a spat that occurred on the playground the day before.

Last week, we learned that three first grade girls, in a small town in Indiana, were suspended from their school because their teacher discovered their plot to kill a fellow classmate. Method undecided, but the choice of weapon had been narrowed down to a knife or gun. A crude map had been drawn of the site where the killing was to take place. We are talking about first grade girls.

But if that were not enough, the next day, two seventh grade girls in Florida, 12 and 13 years old, were charged with plotting to bludgeon and slash the throats of three of their rivals. Authorities found the stash of batteries, knives, and razors that the girls had planned to use.

What will it take for us to heed the signs? To seriously address those sociological issues that have made children comfortable choosing to commit violent acts as casually as they would chose to participate in a sport.

We can blame it on the gory violence brought into the family room by network and cable TV. We can blame the toy and game industry. We can blame irresponsible and absent parents. We can blame violent and crime infested neighborhoods and home environments. We can blame it on pandering politicians who lack the backbone to develop and pass effective legislation as well as enforce the laws already on the books.

But blame is not the issue.

How much more will it take for us to do something about it?

Published April 18, 2000
The Kansas City Star

What Does the American Dream Mean to You?

The notion of the American Dream, that every citizen of this country is free to create a life of prosperity and happiness, has been an iconic one that defines and memorializes what these United States embody. Like Apple Pie, the American Dream is such a part of our collective psyche and culture. Like Apple Pie, it is something we think we want whether we have had the opportunity to taste it, achieve it, or not?

What does the American Dream mean to you? Do you believe it is just an empty patriotic idea or something that is really attainable?

Historically, the notion of the American Dream is almost as old as America itself. It is part of and suppose to define the American experience almost with such weight and importance as the Declaration of Independence, the Bill of Rights, and the U.S. Constitution. Being able to achieve the American Dream is the very embodiment of those sacred documents.

But, like the Declaration of Independence, the Bill of Rights, and U.S. Constitution, does the freedom or opportunity to achieve and live out the American Dream apply equally to everyone? What does the American Dream mean to you? Based on your experience in America to date, do you think you have an equal chance to achieve it, have achieved it, or will be able to?

Some define the American dream in terms of being able to get a good education, finding and growing in a good fulfilling job, owning a home in a good neighborhood, and for many finding the love of his or her life, settling down and having children. For others, finding and achieving the American Dream can be something different entirely.

The American Dream simply means the freedom to pursue whatever endeavor one wishes and be successful at it, whether it is an accomplished artist or architect, baker or barber, clergyman or counselor, driver or dancer, educator or explorer, fireman or farmer, gardener or gymnast, whatever occupation, or profession one can image from A to Z.

Irrespective of race, gender, age, or socioeconomic status, every citizen of these United States should have equal access and opportunity to pursue their American Dream.

In the current educational, economic, political, and social environments, do you think the iconic quest of the American Dream is realistic and achievable?

If so, what is your dream? What does the American Dream mean to you?

Published October 14, 2017
https://janicesellis.com

This Fourth of July Commit to Fight to Save the Soul of America

If you do not like where America seems to be headed, what are you prepared to do about it? This Fourth of July commit to fight of save the soul of America. It is up to us. There is a saying that your actions or inactions either make you a part of the problem or a part of the solution. We the people must fight to save the soul of America.

If you think, at first glance, the statement that we must fight to save the soul of America seem a bit extreme, think again. There are many examples in history where certain propaganda and actions from leaders, along with a silent public, put a society on a slippery slope, which ultimately led to some of the worst human atrocities.

Allowing tyrants, whether self-appointed or inadvertently elected, to run roughshod over a society's values, culture, principles, even long-standing laws of the land, while we watch in disbelief but do nothing is exactly what makes great civilizations disappear.

As we pause to celebrate our republic and the democratic principles and rights that define its existence, the very soul of who we are, we need to ponder whether a lot what has made America great is now at risk. As you celebrate this Fourth of July commit to fight to save the soul of America. The power to do so resides in We, the people.

As you watch the blatant erosion of the quality of leadership, not only in Washington but in capitols all across America, do you think we the people need to use the power of our voices?

Are you concerned that our right as citizens to life, liberty, and the pursuit of happiness is eroding? Based on the divisive rhetoric and proposed policies, are you happy and comfortable with where America seems to be heading?

If not, what are you willing to do about it? We, the people, have the power to determine what America is about, what sets us apart from other countries, and what makes us a great nation, a mediocre or heartless nation. What do you want your homeland to be about? How do you want it to be known to your children, grandchildren?

How do you want America to be recognized in the world, for its goodness or baseness?

The essence, the soul, of a nation is ultimately defined by the values and behavior of its people. During this Fourth of July commit to fight to save the soul of America. We can do that by speaking up, speaking out and committing to vote for the right people with the right values and holding them accountable while they are in office. They must support policies that are consistent with what makes America a good, decent, and great nation—as outlined in our Declaration of Independence.

This Fourth of July commit to fight to save the soul of America.

Published July 3, 2018
https://janicesellis.com

Who and What Does America Stand For?

Who and what does America stand for when it comes to access to healthcare for all of its citizens? That should be a question on the minds of every thoughtful and informed citizens as we watch how the challenges are being handled when it comes to providing affordable and quality health care services.

America brags about being the best nation on earth, the leader of the free world. Can America really continue to lay claim or live up to what such a reputation means? One must ask the question when we consider where America stands compared to other nation in certain categories.

These questions are blatant when it comes to the state of every American citizens having access or being able to afford health care services. There are countries that have better health care systems when it comes to access, affordability and outcomes that we do in the United States.

We need not have to look very far. Just turn to our neighbor to the north, Canada. But it is not just Canada.

A study in 2014 show that the United States approach and provision of healthcare services to its citizens is among the worst among advanced industrialized nations. In addition to Canada, France, Germany, Australia, New Zealand, Norway, Sweden, the United Kingdom and Switzerland, all have better and more efficient healthcare delivery systems. They also out rank the U.S. in terms of quality, the overall healthiness of citizens, and equal access.

Who and what does America stand for should be the question that we all ask when it comes to healthcare services in this country. Who benefits from a broken healthcare system?

How can providing access to affordability and quality healthcare be such a bitter partisan issue where one side has to prevail even if what is proposed is not good for those citizens who are the most in need of those services and the most vulnerable among us—the poor, the sickest, and the elderly.

When most Americans have some coverage through their employer, is policy makers in Washington telling the rest of American citizens to fend for themselves and basically go without primary care, wellness, and prevention services?

We the people must assume the responsibility for voting people in office who seem to either not know or care about what is in the best interest of the citizens they represent.

Who and what does America stand for when it comes to quality and affordable healthcare services?

Published May 4, 2017
https://janicesellis.com

Why Is Donald Trump So Appealing?

Why is Donald Trump so appealing to many Americans, young, middle age, and seniors alike? The answer is neither very simple nor very obvious. It is not just about the state of politics or the economy in the United States today. By most standards, the economy has improved significantly during the last seven years under the Obama administration.

The state of politics? Well, that is a different issue. Yes, many citizens are sick and tired of the stalemate in Washington between President Obama and the Republican dominated Congress. Yes, the vitriol, racist and obstructionist rhetoric spewing from the mouths of Republican Senators and Congressmen.

Why is Donald Trump so appealing? No doubt this seven-year atmosphere has contaminated the political soil and has turned out to be fertile breeding ground for a Donald Trump to rise.

Yes, there is this spoken and unspoken notion that with the growing presence of minorities with all colors and stripes, white America need to take their country back. There is growing fear from the Census Bureau's prediction that within the next twenty to thirty years, the United States will be a nation of minorities. No one group, white, black, or Hispanic, will be in the majority.

There will be a more even distribution of political power if not economic power. This means that those who have dominated this country for more than two hundred years, exercised power and held all other groups at bay, have growing fear and concerns – justifiable or not.

Those are the more obvious reasons. What is less obvious and what we often forget about are the reasons and profiles of those who founded America. Many who immigrated to the new world had grown tired and weary of the government and King of England.

We all recall the rebellion against "taxation without representation," the lack of religious freedom—essentially the absence of many tenets of our Bill of Rights, which comprise the foundation, the very backbone of this country.

But England also took this rebellion as an opportunity to get rid of its dissidents, its rejects. The Statue of Liberty's inscription is legendary: "Give me your tired, your poor, your huddled masses yearning to breathe free, the wretched refuse of your teeming shore. Send these, the homeless, tempest-tossed to me, I lift my lamp beside the golden door!"

Did these words ring true, back then and now, irrespective of the color of your skin? Has that creed been equally applied?

Now, you think about the many reasons why Donald Trump has so much appeal.

Why is Donald Trump so appealing? It is a question worth pondering, looking beneath the surface.

Published March 21, 2016
https://janicesellis.com

World's Strongest Democracy Tested

A lot is riding on the outcome of the 2000 Presidential Election: Ultimately, how Americans will feel about their democracy—how well it works or does not work when its fundamental precept, the right and act of voting, is tested.

What has occurred presents many opportunities to teach, to learn, to improve, to correct and to strengthen our collective resolve.

However, these are not necessarily obvious opportunities in the minds of many. Many voters, no doubt, are feeling frustrated, disenchanted—some disenfranchised because of the unknown status of their—and even angry at what could turn out to be a drawn-out process which could leave a bitter taste in the mouths of many irrespective of the outcome.

We all would like to think that by 5:00 p.m. today we will see some end in sight. That there will be a fair resolution in getting a final tally of votes in Florida and by this Friday, with the overseas absentee ballots firmly in hand and counted, we will know who our President-Elect is, and the country can be about the business of getting on with business.

USING MY WORD POWER

We are all eager to get back to a national sense of normalcy, accept whoever is the victor, put aside the divisive aspects of our partisanship and begin to work together for the greater good of the country and its citizenry. Maybe even have a normal holiday season, capping it off with the anticipation of an invigorating January Presidential inauguration ceremony that will inspire our patriotic verve and resolve and once again kindle within us thoughts of what our country can continue to become.

Whether we get that since of satisfaction by this Friday or not, we all, as American citizens, should be confident that it will ultimately come.

Our democracy is strong enough to past this test and will be the better for it.

In many ways, what has happened can be perceived as the greatest peacetime shot in the arm, for democracy, in a long time. Usually, a country's sense of patriotism and collective verve is felt strongest when it is called into war.

Perhaps this is an internal war, of sorts, of the people's will.

Irrespective of how we might feel about the count, recount, and other counts of the votes in Florida or additional states that may be brought into the fray before it is all said and done, there are a few conclusions that are irrefutable:

- It is clear that each individual vote does and can make a difference in the determination of both the impact of the Electoral College, the popular vote, and therefore, ultimately who becomes President of the United States.

- The indeterminate outcome of this election presents an excellent opportunity to teach a great civic lesson to our children on how our democracy works and the importance of their participatory and vigilant roles in it.

- If more nonvoters and unregistered citizens had voted, perhaps the outcome would have been more definitive, with one candidate clearly becoming the winner.

- Whether the new Congress rises to the occasion or not, this election provides one of the greatest reasons ever to revisit how elections are held in this country from the role of the electoral college to which day elections should be held and how votes should be cast and counted.

But, unfortunately, we know that there will be those who will use this unique occurrence as an opportunity to become even more cynical about the political process. Many citizens may not see the value in their vote. Many will choose to believe that there is more manipulation and mischief than there actually is. Many will use the occasion to become even more entrenched in their partisan leanings, feeding on the most destructive stereotypical views to achieve a psychological safe political place.

USING MY WORD POWER

In the end, let us hope that cynicism and partisan bickering will be held in check by the tenets of a democracy that have withstood greater tests than this, and that the flames of democracy will burn more brilliantly and brighter than ever, for /{more/} Americans than ever.

What other outcome could there be for the strongest democracy in the world?

None other.

Published November 14, 2000
The Kansas City Star

Part Two

Politics and the People

American politics is often filled with both order and chaos, and defined as effective and ineffective. By the very nature of its founding and most sacred documents—the Declaration of Independence, Bill of Rights, and the Constitution—America and the political process require adherence to the principles and laws outlined in them. Participatory politics and the will of the people go hand-in-hand. This collection of commentaries examines some of the temporal and lasting issues that impact life in America and how they have been addressed, and are being addressed, by politics and the people.

Prelude: Sample of Earliest Writings

Politics As A Spectator Sport

Low voter turnout in elections, whether at the local or national level, is indicative of politics becoming a spectator sport for the majority of Americans.

Politics, for most of us, is a passing parade—a series of pictures in the mind placed there by the television news, newspapers, and magazines, pictures which create a moving panorama, taking place in a world we never quite touch, yet one we come to fear or cheer—often with passion but only rarely with action. We are content to leave the operation of our government to others.

Being a spectator is proper when we are not expected to participate. But failing to participate, when we should, is an injustice to ourselves and others who depend on us. We, in effect, forfeit not only our right to influence outcomes but also our right to criticize them once they have occurred without our efforts. We, as residents of a city, county, state, and nation, should influence and determine how government operates—on all levels—by being concerned about how our tax dollars are spent, how federal funds are handled, and how other important matters that directly impact the quality of our lives are dealt with.

But as it stands, we have become too apathetic and too content to leave crucial aspects of our own destiny to the passing whims and feelings of others. We are content to sit around the bar or the fireplace and complain about higher taxes, governmental red tape, and too much governmental interference in our private lives (from the education of our children to how we run our businesses, to keeping a record on our social and private lives). Yet discussing these problems at the bar or around the fireplace is not voicing our opinion where it counts.

We elect officials. We give them their jobs. They should hear our concerns and act on behalf of our needs and wishes.

> *– This spot was first delivered on January 20, 1975, and was re-aired on February 4, 1976, as the U.S. presidential campaign and many congressional and state campaigns were getting into full swing.*
> WISN Radio, ABC Affiliate

Faith Plays An Integral Role in American Politics

A cursory review of American history shows the central role God and religion played and continue to play in our politics.

From the Revolutionary War to the formation and drafting of our most sacred national documents, God and religious principles are boldly infused throughout.

The phrase "separation of church and state" is not found in the Constitution.

Instead, it prohibits federal and state governments from nationalizing any religion, creating a national church, and favoring one religion over the other.

The misuse and hypocrisy come into play with the sporadic denials or discriminate efforts to separate or invoke the use of God and religion to support or defeat one policy position or another.

Tensions between separation of church and state and the roles God and religion play in shaping public policy are seen in the ongoing debate around issues like abortion, same sex marriage and LGBTQ rights.

But perhaps the most notable example of church and state working hand-in-hand is the role religious leaders and churches play in our elections.

There is a reason why candidates tailor their messages to appeal to certain religious doctrines and beliefs to gain support and to solidify a voting bloc.

There is a reason why candidates go to Black churches to make their case. The support of Black congregants can determine the outcome of an election.

There are blurred lines and porous borders between church and state, which are often crossed in our politics and daily lives in both obvious and subtle ways to gain an advantage when promoting an agenda.

So why the pretense that never the twain shall meet, let alone mix — when they meet and mix all the time? Are we being hypocrites when we yell foul in one instance and turn a blind eye in another?

Perhaps the confusion is between separation of church and state and the role God and religion play in our institutions, traditions, and our daily lives.

The founders were very clear and deliberate about the centrality of God and religion in the vision, mission and purpose in forming America.

Some of our most endearing patriotic songs invoke the presence and blessings of God, from "America the Beautiful" to "Battle Hymn of the Republic" to "My Country, Tis of Thee."

Songs, and music, have a way of reaching our better selves. In these divisive times, revisiting them, humming and singing along could go a long way in reviving a positive and healthy patriotic spirit.

But the integral relationship between God, church and state doesn't stop there.

Even our currency proudly displays and proclaims, "In God We Trust."

The role religion has played in the developmental history of this country is everywhere.

As we witness how low our public dialogue has sunk, the increasing inhumane conduct toward each other and the contrived displays of righteous indication by those same perpetrators, one could conclude that they are signs that America is losing, or indeed has lost, its moral compass.

Just as a person's faith is linked when it comes to advocating for candidates, legislation and laws, they could be even more valuable in reclaiming what is honorable and good for American society overall.

A few examples come to mind.

Maybe following the Biblical teaching, "Love thy neighbor as thyself"— or as the non-religious would say "treat each other as we would want to be treated"— would bring civility and respect back in our public discourse.

Maybe we will ensure that everyone, regardless of race or gender, are treated with the same dignity, respect and believe implicitly that they are entitled to all inalienable rights.

Maybe fighting for the care of the poor and orphaned children among us would have as much priority as protecting the unborn.

Just maybe.

The foundation is there. God and Biblical principles have been embraced and adopted in our most sacred documents, our patriotic songs, our public ceremonies and traditions honoring our flag and country.

Religious leaders and their congregations all across America have been and continue to be actively engaged in the political process.

There is more to be gained by fully embracing the connection between church and state, when it comes to defining us as Americans, than continuing the practice of selective separation when it is convenient.

The church-state connection, in many ways, is what has determined America's character and set her apart from the very beginning.

We need not be hypocritical about how that connection could be applied to improve our relationship with our fellowman and country.

Published March 7, 2022
Missouri Independent.com

Negative Political Ads Pollute and Debase the Political Process of Our Democracy

When you hear that more than twenty million dollars were spent in negative advertising in the Florida Presidential Primary, it is little wonder that the average citizen thinks our election process has become a joke, a necessary evil. But is that perception and resignation doing us more harm than good?

The *body politic* impacts our lives in all its aspects—from where our children go to school, what money is left from our paycheck to improve our standard of living, to the quality and bacteria-free food we put on our tables for our loved ones to eat. If one just stops to think, it becomes abundantly clear that decisions made by politicians every day, at every level of government are eventually felt in our daily lives. There are few or no exceptions.

But too often we as citizens do not want to have anything to do with it. And little wonder when you look at the election and political process today. What is allowed in terms of false, distorted, and negative advertising during campaigns is a travesty, an insult to democracy and the fullness of its meaning.

Unfortunately, with the behavior of Congress and now candidates on the campaign trail, whenever we hear the word politics, anyone of a number of things probably come to mind: the often grandiose promises candidates make to get elected or re-elected to office, only to forget or ignore those same promises once in office. Or we think of the strategies, tactics and contributions big business put in place to leverage influence and get concessions from governmental entities at the average citizen's expense. Look at the political packs and their ability to put millions of dollars into a campaign to influence the outcome through negative and false political ads.

These practices are further confounded by the constant parade of elected officials lured by the temptation to line their own pockets, or those of their friends and family, or they insist on indulging in unethical and unsavory behavior. The profile of the current Congress shows the wealth—whether members came with it or accumulated it since being elected.

Whatever the impressions that the average citizen holds, suffice it to say they generally carry negative overtones because of the way much of the political activities are carried out today at all levels of government. The bad or evil deeds of the few, too often, overshadow the good of the majority.

When the great Greek philosopher, Plato, wrote the seminal book, *The Republic*, on government and the role of citizens in governing, politics was not only an honorable and patriotic process, but it also represented the heart and soul of a healthy society. Politics meant those deliberations, active, sometimes vigorous, and lively discussions, among citizens who diligently searched to determine and promote the greatest good for the greatest number with each policy decision made.

Two things are fundamentally different in our society today and they are mirrored at all levels of government. First, as the population increases, citizens' interest and participation in the welfare of their government decrease. Fewer people bother to vote. Many cannot tell you who their city, state or national elected officials are.

Secondly, consistent low voter turnout represents the feeling of powerlessness, and perhaps unconcern, on the part of many of our citizens. Somehow, too many citizens feel that their involvement or vote will not make much of a difference anyway. This deep-seated feeling of impotency, if not helplessness, is the most insidious and potentially harmful trend of all—particularly for those who are already at a disadvantage economically, socially, and educationally.

The consequences of non-participation in politics and the political process are grave and lasting. Just think about it. Many elected officials do not feel obliged to represent, protect or fight for the interest of those who did bother to cast a vote. It is difficult enough for voters to hold many elected officials accountable once they get in office.

The critical question in the upcoming elections is: Can we afford to continue to be a spectator rather than a participant, irrespective of how disgusting some aspects of the process have become?

Our political process seems to be increasingly sliding to a place where negativity and incivility reign, but it is an integral and inextricable part of our lives. We cannot cut it out. Our apathy or disenchantment with it will not make it go away.

Then isn't our only viable alternative to get involved and influence it? Stop the negativity? Change it?

Published February 1, 2012
USAonRace.com

New United States Congress Represents US

A new United States Congress has been sworn in — the 113th — to represent us, we the people. But so did the last Congress and all that have gone before. So why are we not holding them accountable to make decisions that is in our best interest?

Every two years, we have the opportunity to select someone to go to Washington to make sure that the issues that affect the quality of life in our city, community, and household are taken into consideration when policy decisions are made, and dollars are spent. But we repeatedly fail to hold the Congress we elected accountable.

Question: After casting your vote, what have you done or what will you do to ensure that your Congressional representative is looking out for you and not his or her largest contributor?

The outcome of this last election should be evidence that money is not all powerful. The people's vote was the power that ruled the day with the outcome of the U.S. Presidential election, as well as many contested elections in the U.S. Senate and House of Representatives despite the unprecedented amount of money spent.

The outcomes should trump the growing cynicism about whether our political process works.

But the elections outcome was just the beginning. Our real work as citizens has just begun. We must be actively engaged in holding Congress accountable.

If you have any doubt, just review the lack of performance of the last United States Congress. On last Friday, it faded into the annals of history as one of the worst, most ineffective, "Peoples House" since the founding of the Republic. We failed abysmally in holding Congress accountable.

But really, who is to blame? We, the people. The United State Congress represents us. We elected them and left them to bask in their personal and partisan bickering, while we the people, endured high unemployment, looked inept as a nation, and lost enviable credibility on the world stage.

America aired its dirty underwear.

There was a perpetual parade of disrespect of the Office of President—unprecedented in American history. But then so is Barack Obama as the first African American President.

Getting the nation's fiscal house in order took a second seat to the ardent and strident efforts to maintain irrational and antiquated political philosophies, while the nation's and to a great extent the world's economic health continued to decline.

To secure the availability of healthcare services for most Americans took an act of the Supreme Court, which was dubious at best. But a dubious act turns out to be better than a negative one.

The only way to avoid a repeat of the performance of the last United States Congress is to hold the new Congress accountable.

Will we? Or will it be business as usual, while all we do is sit around and complain?

If we fail at holding Congress accountable and we get another two years like the last two, we have only ourselves to blame.

We might as well become a large cheering squad on the sidelines, because with our inaction we are essentially saying: You, go Congress!

Published January 7, 2013
USAonRace.com

Beware of the Danger of the Undertow

Despite the unprecedented turn out of new and young voters during the last presidential election, which resulted in Barack Obama becoming the first African American president, there is still pervasive cynicism among young people about our government and the political process.

From where does such entrenched cynicism come?

With the advent of the internet, are the younger generations relying too much on snippets and summaries of historical events as well as contemporary ones that are shaping the future direction of this country?

Is there too much reliance on the often unsubstantiated positions and edicts of political pundits and "talking heads," especially those who feed on the sensational and daily ratings to ensure their own survival amid the crowded cacophonous airways.

Unfortunately, this undercurrent of cynicism is not just among young people. Evidence abounds that it transcends age, sex, race, ethnicity, and economic class and is only surpassed by the swell of reasons flowing from government and its leaders—at all levels. From the White House to the State House. From the county seat to the city council. From an appointed board to an elected board.

You can hardly pick up the newspaper or turn on the evening news without learning of the latest transgression, proven, or alleged, committed by someone who is supposed to be a protector of the public's best interest and a keeper of the public trust.

As President Obama and Congress grapple with some of the most important issues confronting us today—health care reform, the war in Afghanistan, an ailing economy with high unemployment—we cannot seem to escape the new episodes of wrongdoing by veteran senators or congressmen. And the plot is all too common as we hear about yet another act of financial greed or sexual indiscretion

It does not stop there. We do not have the luxury of playing the delusional game of, "Oh, that's them, not us." Nor can we claim that corruption and abuse of power are commonplace only at the higher levels of government. We have only to think of the indictments and fall of leaders in our state governments, our city councils—even school boards.

When we look at the pervasiveness of immoral, unethical, and illegal behavior among our elected and appointed officials and the negative undercurrent it breeds, we must search our individual and collective souls to uncover the reasons why this problem persists. Does the blame lie solely with the perpetrators? Or must the blame be shared by us, the public, for our continual tolerance through our silence and lack of demonstrative steps that would clearly convey our outrage?

There are so many questions to grapple with when we see our elected officials consumed, and often dethroned, by scandal. How much of it is contrived by political enemies or opposing factions? How much is due to a character flaw or a lack of a moral center of strong ethical values?

More importantly, how does the public sort it all? Where does truth lie? How are we able to recognize truth when we see or hear it? As our spirits are being zapped by the latest revelation, we are expected to keep a clear mind, discerning truth as we watch and listen to the spin pundits weave and intertwine fact and fiction so freely--masking it all as possible truth.

It is little wonder that public trust and confidence in our government and its leaders are at an all-time low almost at every level. How could anyone possibly expect our citizens to stay engaged, avoiding being drowned by cynicism?

But, like the good swimmer, we as concerned citizens, must stay in tuned, remain watchful. An experienced and knowledgeable swimmer knows that the undertow can be deadly; and it is wise to stay attentive during the swim, remaining close to the beach or near the shore.

And like a good student of history, we must learn from and avoid the mistakes of the past. A student of history knows that many great civilizations were destroyed from within; and therefore, one must look amid the ruins and identify the negative internal forces that caused the collapse. Disenchantment is often the number one culprit.

But we cannot be good students with our eyes only glued to the television or the Internet where almost anyone can post a thought, incomplete information and position it as the ultimate and final truth. We must commit to dig deeper on our own to get to the real sources. Television, radio, and the Internet with all of its communication tentacles (U-Tube, Twitter, Facebook, and yes the Blog) should be just the beginning of our quest for knowledge and truth around any issue that concerns us.

If we do not resume this kind of ownership of the information we consume and the impact it has on our actions, then it is very easy to become a cynical bystander.

The political undertow of cynicism claims another every time someone tunes out our democratic process.

Published October 14, 2009
USAonRace.com

Awesome Responsibility of Presidential Leadership

There are few roles that match the awesome responsibility of presidential leadership, especially the position of President of United States. An American President not only is leader of this nation, but in many respects, he or she is the leader of the free world.

One of the first responsibilities is to always function and make decisions that are in the best interest of the America, and the welfare of her citizens. The President should never be a divider, but a unifier.

America is not an oligarchy, ruled by a despot or dictator, military junta, or regime. It is a democratic republic controlled by the people. The president and every member of Congress are elected to do the will of the people, not to promote their own self-interests.

What we are witnessing today from the highest offices in our land is not just shameful and hurtful, and having a negative impact on our country today, if it is not stopped, it will define our quality of life for years and decades to come.

This dysfunctional and detrimental moment in American history can only lead to further erosion and decent of our honor and dignity. Hopefully, it will be an awakening of the need to reclaim, restore, preserve, and promote what has made America great.

Today, too many elected officials fail to acknowledge and uphold the awesome responsibility of presidential leadership. It begs the question why they ran so hard and spend so much money to get elected, only to abdicate their responsibilities and not speak out against obvious wrongs.

This is a public service reminder to all elected officials: You were elected because the people who voted for you believed in what you told them and trusted that you would do and work for those things you promised. If everyone kept their oath, a dishonest despot could not survive, let alone thrive.

Our Democratic Republic was set up with checks and balances to ensure that the Executive, Legislative, and Judicial branches carry out their responsibilities as outlined in the Constitution.

Also, on a basic, decency, humane level: Have you heard of the old sayings, "Your word, certainly your oath, is your bond?" What about the simple recognition that, "Words matter?"

From the President to the Senators and Representatives, we the people voted you in office to do what is in the best interest of America and its citizens.

The awesome responsibility of Presidential leadership should be leading by example.

That being said, America where are we?

Published October 3, 2019
https://janicesellis/blog

The People Must Demand Civility From Congress, Now

We must start now to reclaim a civil electoral and public policy process. And it begins with demanding an end to the current charade taking place in Congress. We cannot wait until the 2012 elections. If we do not see effective and clear changes prior to those elections, then those we choose to vote for or against should be very clear.

The powerful Congressman, Tip O'Neill, was known for his declaration that "All Politics is Local." He authored a book with the same title. What is the state of politics and the public policy process—whether at the local, state, or national level? Just look around beginning with your community, your city, and beyond.

For those of you who may not have heard of or remember, Tip O'Neill, Thomas Phillip "Tip" O'Neill, Jr. was considered an *American* politician. O'Neill, an outspoken liberal Democrat in common political parlance, was one of the most influential members to have served in the U.S. Congress. Representing two congressional districts in Massachusetts during his 34 years in the House of Representatives, he rose to the positions of Majority Whip, Majority Leader, and was one of the longest-serving Speakers of the House under three presidential administrations (Gerald Ford, Jimmy Carter, and Ronald Regan).

O'Neill had it right. Serving the people who elected him was his first priority. He clearly knew and practiced the art of compromise to have survived that long in a leadership position during both Democratic and Republican administrations.

What did he know that our current members of Congress do not seem to know or understand?

Tip O'Neill did not remain an effective voice and force by playing to the sound and fury of the rancorous and raucous few. Even being from Massachusetts, if the vocal nouveau Tea Partiers were in the minority, they would not have controlled his actions in Congress.

Fast forward to politics and the political environment today, Tip O'Neill must be rolling in his resting place. The rancor is palpable. The blatant acts and bursts of disrespect of the Office of President and the Halls of Congress are there for the world to witness. How did we get to this place in American political history?

Did the election of the first black President bring this unprecedented unguarded behavior to the forefront? It certainly begs the question.

Economic times are tough. They have been tough before—even worse by some standards. While this current administration and Congress have not been able to forge policies that could bring about real relief, the actions of administrations and Congresses past share the blame and responsibility.

So, what really spun the contemporaneous Tea Party movement? Greed on Wall Street did not just rear its ugly head. The unfair tax policies and tax codes did not just come into existence. We did not just amass trillions of dollars of debt. Twelve million illegal Mexican immigrants did not just invade our soil in the last two years.

Why has such an unprecedented visceral, cancerous, obstinate posture taken over the current members of Congress? Why are they comfortable ignoring the will of the people?

So, what should the people do? Use the greatest power they have: The vote and their power of persuasion to get others to vote.

We are bombarded daily with aspiring candidates who want to become President of the United States. Soon we will be bombarded with candidates at all levels of government asking us to entrust them to make decisions at our behest, in our best interest.

Do not be fooled. Do not be gullible. Do not be taken with the self-serving slants and slogans. We must look carefully at those who currently hold these highly important offices as well as those who seek to replace them.

Much too much is riding on our vote—every one of them. Just as we decide how to invest our money, how we choose in whom to invest our vote is going to make a great difference in the future we can expect.

At a minimum, we should expect a return to civility—a return to putting the interest of the people above all other personal and partisan agendas.

It is not too early to pay very close attention to see who can deliver the greatest return on the people's business...

Published October 29, 2011
USAonRace.com

Big Government Bailouts and Big Executive Bonuses: Longing for the Lessons of Horatio Alger

The President and Congress demanding no bonus payments, pay cuts, and claw backs of some of the executives of companies who received big government bailouts—and continue to benefit at the egregious exploitation of consumers, taxpayers, investors, and employees, alike—is just not enough.

Horatio Alger, most assuredly, is turning over in his grave with the "rags-to-riches" rise of the executives of some of the nation's largest corporations and the greedy, fraudulent, and pernicious way in which they have gotten there.

Alger, certainly, cannot be resting in peace.

Alger, during the post-Civil War era, wrote over a hundred books extolling the virtue of hard work, perseverance, and honesty. The heroes of his books had strong ethical and moral values. They exhibited kindness and generosity on their road to success.

Even though more that 250 million copies of his books have been sold worldwide, perhaps a few of them need to be required reading for present and future executives and the boards that are responsible for governing them.

A few relevant books for the times in which we find ourselves come to mind: *Fame and Fortune; Ragged Dick; Risen from the Ranks; Brave and Bold*; and *Abraham Lincoln.*

Alger's books really have lessons for us all. And it may be well for our lawmakers to dust off a few of his books and read them for moral strength as they deliberate about what is the appropriate punishment for corporate thievery.

Despite their party affiliation, elected officials in Washington need to exercise moral courage with the enforcement of strong laws that will mete out the right punishment for the, excesses, abuses and crimes that have been perpetrated against ordinary and trusting citizens—many of whom still believe in the Horatio Alger way of doing things.

With all the financial bailouts and assistance extended to some of those same perpetrators born by hard working taxpayers, current elected officials have a moral duty and obligation to do more than demand pay cuts, claw backs or no bonuses.

As we assess the candidates running for elective office in 2010, we need to ask them a direct question, "What will you do to ensure that employees, investors and their families are not exploited by illegal and unscrupulous business practices?'" And we need to listen very carefully to the answers.

In the short term, not only has unsuspecting older Americans been robbed of hard-earned money they had depended on for retirement, but other workers have seen college funds for their kids dissipate. Money saved to buy their first home evaporated.

If our President and members of Congress fail to do the right thing, it could seriously undermine not only our free enterprise way of life, but it could also mortgage our future because young people who are watching may find it difficult to continue to believe in some of the fundamental tenets that keep our Republic strong.

And no matter how many Horatio Alger books they read, they may easily conclude that they refer to a bygone way of life, with characters whose belief systems and moral values no longer are applicable in a business world that seem devoid of them.

What a tragedy, should this occur.

Each year, the Horatio Alger Association of Distinguished Americans host an annual awards dinner in our nation's capital. The 2010 recipients will be announced in December. The Horatio Alger Award is given to ten Americans who have made outstanding contributions in their fields. Since its inception in 1947, many elected officials and business have been honored.

The Association offers many programs to bring together Horatio Alger heroes of today with those of tomorrow. Young people are offered opportunities to explore first-hand how America's free enterprise system works. During the National Scholars Conference, which is held in Washington, D.C., students are able to see how our executive, legislative and judicial branches of government work.

If we are successful in preventing a melt-down of our economic infrastructure, participant in future Horatio Alger conferences will have much to discuss and many lessons to learn. If our elected official and justice system have done their jobs, hopefully the real corporate crooks will be in jail and systems will be in place to make it difficult for those who are so criminally inclined to run amok again.

It would do us well to perhaps hold Horatio Alger workshops for young people all across America to teach them what constitutes a good code of business conduct. To remind them that despite what they see in many of the corporate leaders, there is a right and decent way to go from "rags-to-riches" and it is not always about how much personal wealth you amass. It also involves how you help and enrich the lives of others.

There are many elected officials and business leaders who exemplify the very values and that need to be passed on to future generations.

Will the Horatio Alger Distinguished Americans please stand up?

Published October 22, 2009
USAonRace.com

Perils of Not Knowing Your History

The perils of not knowing your history can be really detrimental, even catastrophic. Making decisions in a vacuum, without any perspective, is tantamount to flying blindfolded. A major crash is inevitable. This is true at an individual level. It is certainly true at a broader level, whether we are talking about the community in which we live, the city, state, and our nation.

There is real truth in the adage, "If you do not know where you have been, you cannot have a clear picture of where you should go." How can you? From what perspective? Not knowing your history makes one vulnerable to making poor choices. It makes one vulnerable to following whims, impulses, and others who may lead you down a destructive path.

One has only to think of what their life would be like if they did not have a clue about their family history, which includes biological lineage of parents, grandparents, their way of life, and the conditions of their lives that resulted in both trials and triumphs.

If you think there are perils of not knowing your history, imagine the tremendous risk when the leaders of our cities, our states, and our nation do not have a sound understanding of the history, the principles, laws, and forces that have played critical roles in where they are today.

While knowledgeable leaders are important at every level of government, knowing the history of this nation is most important of all. Making policy decisions, both domestic and foreign, without a fundamental understanding of American history, our laws, values, strengths, vulnerabilities, and more importantly our future direction, is the ultimate in recklessness.

When you see what is developing in our nation's capital, you are witnessing the tragic results of what happens when those in charge are both ignorant and irreverent when it comes to America's history, values, and rule of law. We are watching the perils of not knowing our history unfold in our very eyes.

The brazen and reckless behaviors of the president, some members of the Senate and the House of Representatives are blatant examples of a lack of knowledge and appreciation of the experiences that have shaped America during the last two hundred plus years. This is utter disregard of how far this country has come.

How can they possible lead the nation into a positive future, both at home and abroad?

Shouldn't every caring American be gravely concerned?

Published October 10, 2019
https://janicesellis.com

Healthcare Insurance for Millions of Americans At Risk

The renewed efforts to repeal the Affordable Healthcare Act, commonly referred to as Obamacare, is putting healthcare insurance for millions of Americans at risk. Why do you think that President Trump and Republican lawmakers are calling once again to repeal the Affordable Healthcare Act?

Why is the effort to provide access to health care services for millions of Americans continue to be caught in the crosshairs of partisan politics? It begins with how it is commonly referred to: Obamacare rather than the Affordable Healthcare Act. The former reference is more negative and incendiary, and the latter is more positive and comforting.

To repeal or not to repeal the healthcare policy seems to be an issue that is used when it is politically expedient, a recurring political football, which puts healthcare insurance for millions of Americans at risk. Many of these Americans would not have access to needed healthcare services, otherwise.

There are more than twenty-eight million (28,000,000+) Americans enrolled in the Affordable Healthcare Plan or

Obamacare. This new effort to repeal Obamacare is not offering anything to replace it. So, what is driving this latest effort? Is it simple because passage of the Affordable Healthcare Act was a major accomplishment of President Barack Obama?

Is hating and trying to undo everything that President Obama achieved worth putting healthcare insurance for millions of Americans at risk? Many of those insured have pre-existing and chronic health conditions. Yet, the same legislators calling to get rid of Obamacare are not offering anything, any plan, to put in its place.

So how are the millions of Americans currently enrolled in Obamacare supposed to feel? What options will they have? What kind of hardship and anxiety must this political football be causing?

If more Americans are able to get health care through the Affordable Healthcare Act, why not choose to seek fixes and improvements to make it better instead of trying to undo it? A policy so needed, and so broad cannot not be perfect out of the gate. There are always things to change and work out as more experience is gained.

Improve upon Obamacare rather than repeal it. Repealing it without having something better to replace it puts healthcare insurance for millions of American at risk.

Shouldn't all Americans have access to quality healthcare?

Published March 20, 2019
https://janicesellis.com/blog

How Has Electing a Black Man As President Impacted Race Relations?

About this time four years ago, many people did not believe Barack Obama would be the Democratic Party nominee for President of the United States over his formidable rival, Hillary Clinton. But disbelief slowly gave way to belief, and ultimate seminal hope and euphoria when he ultimately became President Barack Obama. At least for some.

There were those who optimistically believed that America had truly turned a page in history in terms of improving race relations, finally putting to rest many ugly bigoted beliefs, prejudicial practices, and decades of discrimination that had persisted despite the laws and policies that had been passed. But there were also those equally determined to hang on the racial divides, and they have played out in one major way since President Barack Obama took office.

A new *Newsweek* poll confirms that since the election of Barack Obama, many people believe that not only has his election not helped race relations but may have done more to widen the racial divide. According to the poll, "nearly 60 percent of Americans are now convinced that race relations have either deteriorated or stagnated" since President Obama took office.

This opinion is prevalent among whites and blacks.

But should we be surprised. The vestiges of racism and the conditions that bred and continue to breed its perennial presence were implanted and nurtured in every aspect of American society long before Barack Obama was elected president. One could argue, based upon history, and based upon the rancor that has played out during his presidency, that his election was an aberration. That electing a black person will be a "norm" that will continue to elude us for generations to come.

The divides and perceptions of them among blacks and whites run deep.

The poll confirms that given the same scenarios, blacks and whites come away with different conclusions. For example, while both black and whites can agree that racial stereotyping still occur, they disagree how it affects black people's lives. When it comes to affordable housing, 70 percent of whites thinks that blacks have an equal chance of buying one compared to only 35 percent of blacks believing the same. Only 25 percent of blacks believe that they receive equal treatment in the job market compared to 70 percent of whites. And when it comes to police and the court system, 84 percent of whites believe that blacks receive the same treatment as whites compared to 52 percent of blacks.

With such opposite views based upon life experience, how do we hope to ever get to a place where we work together to achieve meaningful and lasting improvement in relations among the races?

How?

If President Obama gets re-elected, should improving race relations be high among his priorities to address during the next four years?

Published April 20, 2012
USAonRace.com

How Will Trump Govern?

How will Trump govern should he be elected the next President of the United States? He certainly will not be able to govern by edict. He cannot make a policy declaration, and it is then automatically enacted. But this is what he is portraying on the campaign trail.

And, if his supporter truly understood how our government works, they would know that he is basically spewing hot air. He throws out things he would do should he become President that are not only unconstitutional, but he cannot do without approval from both houses of Congress.

So, will the new Congress be a majority of Trumpees and Trumpetts? Will members of the Republican Party along with some independents and disillusioned democrats elect members of Congress who share Donald Trump's views? Are such candidates even running?

Will members of the current Congress, both in the House and Senate, who will still be in office after the 2016 election become Trump minions and proponents of Trumpisms? Will they try to advance legislation that would put some of his ill-conceived and non-factual pronouncements in place for America and Americans to live by?

Doubtful. Very doubtful. And God forbid. So, how will Trump govern?

Trump supporters, while clearly frustrated with the current state of our government need to at least bother to understand the United States Constitution and how this Republic works. First it is a democracy not a dictatorship or an oligarchy. We abide by the policies and rules of three branches of government: judicial, legislative, and executive, not by the demands of a dictator, demagogue, or oligarch.

Democracy means that the will of the majority of the people rules. Not the desires of one man or the few. How will Trump govern?

Talking tough and big, making false promises that cannot possibly be implemented is not only grossly misleading, but very dangerous. Trump is preying upon those Americans who are not only frustrated, fearful, and angry, but very uninformed and misinformed. They should ask, should he be elected, how will Trump govern.

The demagoguery, anger, ignorance, and fear that Trump is advancing potentially make for non-productive and potentially destructive actions and policies. Ones that America and rational Americans cannot afford to approve and live by.

Published December 8, 2015
https://janicesellis.com

Coronavirus Is Not Only Infecting and Killing but Exposing

As we, as a nation, struggle to deal with a health care system under siege and an economy on a steep decline, one thing is certain. Coronavirus is not only infecting and killing but exposing a lot of issues that need to be addressed. What colossal conditions to be faced and, hopefully, lessons to be learned, despite this tragic ordeal.

The long-term physical, mental, economic, and social well-being of Americans and the nation depends on facing facts, truths, and realities. This deep introspection and acknowledgement of some painful truths must occur at every level of government, business, and the public.

We only have to listen to a modicum of news to know that the United States was woefully unprepared to deal with coronavirus despite what we saw occurring in other parts of the world. Our leaders persisted in ignoring multiple warnings from multiple sources. What has resulted is the devastating reality that coronavirus is not only infecting and killing but exposing major inequities.

Those inequities include the alarming fact that many hospitals, nursing homes and front-line workers do not have the basic medical and personal equipment to take care of the flood of infected people that they are exposed to on an hourly and daily basis.

Those inequities include those individuals and small businesses that can least afford it no longer have an income or a way to make a living. Many have no idea how they will recover.

Those inequities include many school-age children left vulnerable who count on schools and teachers for not only learning, but also for much needed nurturing and daily meals because they come from sub-par living homes and living conditions. Coronavirus is not only infecting and killing but exposing, once again, the plight of the poor and disenfranchised among us.

While coronavirus has no respect of age, gender, race, or socioeconomic status when it comes to people being infected and dying, blacks are becoming infected and dying at a much higher rate than any other group across America. In some places, among those becoming infected and dying 40, 50, and as many as 70 percent of those are black. Why?

Because blacks still disproportionately are poorer, lack access to health care, and they fill many of the low-paying frontline jobs. There are those among us who would like to ignore or pretend that America does not have a poverty or racial problem. But this healthcare crisis is saying otherwise. Coronavirus is not only infecting and killing but exposing conditions that still need to be addressed.

Once we get through this crisis, will the leadership and will we demand that these long-standing conditions be addressed? Those conditions include all Americans having access to health care insurance, the level of readiness of the public health care system to combat epidemics and pandemics. What real steps will be taken to address poverty and racial inequities that continue to exist? After we survive this crisis, then what?

Published April 17, 2020
https://janicesellis.com

Coronavirus Should Not Interfere With Elections

If America conducted elections during the Civil War and World War II, the Coronavirus should not interfere with elections taking place now, and especially the Presidential Election in November. There is ample time and a number of options that can be put in place now and the coming months.

The Federal Election system need not be caught flat-footed in ensuring that citizens will be able to vote in November because of failing of invest and preparing viable options for elections to take place in every state. Learn from the Public Health system, which was woefully unprepared to handle the coronavirus, because of a lack of preparation and adequate funding.

The massive spread of the virus and the crippling impact it is having on the economy and every aspect of American life could have been significantly minimized if not avoided had the Public Health System had a plan in place for such a pandemic. There have been decades of neglect and underfunding in resources, medical equipment, and personnel that could have been mobilized for such a time as this.

If the Federal and State Election system begin now putting a plan and options in place that will ensure that every eligible citizen will be able to vote, the coronavirus should not interfere with elections. Elections should be able to take place in towns, cities, and states all across America.

We are already getting warning signals during the Presidential primaries. Several states, Georgia, Louisiana, and Ohio postponed their primary elections because of fears about the coronavirus. Clearly, the health and well-being of citizens should be the priority. But why is it necessary to have to make such a choice?

Many states have already implemented voting by mail. Many others have extended early voting options to everyone without restrictions. Absentee ballots have long been used in nursing homes, the military, and other situations where voters are unable to vote in person. These and other options should be more readily available as options for all eligible voters. The coronavirus should not interfere with elections, especially the November Presidential election.

Congress should pass legislation now with the needed funding to allow the election system to implement options that will ensure that every American can vote. Based on current projections, the country could still be reeling from this global pandemic. If not in a massive way, we certainly could be experiencing a weak and feeble recovery.

USING MY WORD POWER

To President Trump and Congress, please prepare our election system to keep our democracy strong amid this health crisis. This health crisis should be our lesson about the need for and importance of advance preparation. The coronavirus should not interfere with elections, which could further cripple our American way of life.

Published March 18, 2020
https://janicesellis.com

Coronavirus Presents Great Opportunities to Become Closer

While social distancing is being urged as one of the most effective ways to prevent more infections, the coronavirus presents great opportunities to become closer to each other.

First and foremost, it presents an opportunity for world leaders to put nationalism in its proper perspective and come together to share information and other resources to bring global healing in light of this aggressive, deadly, and debilitating pandemic.

But there are many things we can do, as individuals, within our areas of daily influence. Could it be that while being encouraged to stay at home and to work from home, it provides a great opportunity to reconnect with and help family members, friends, and neighbors—near and far?

Contemporary culture and our ways of life have too often required or demanded that we forego nurturing some of the most important relationships. Job demands often rob parents of quality time with their spouse and kids. Those demands often leave less time and energy to interact with other family members—siblings, cousins. Neighbors? Too often, we hardly know their names.

The coronavirus presents great opportunities to become closer with these important people in our lives as we maintain social distancing. Where we are unable to have direct in-person contact, technology affords us many options to stay connected.

The rapid arrival and spread of the coronavirus have certainly changed things. The mass closure of schools and businesses has abruptly forced us all to adjust and make changes in our daily lives. Whether welcomed or not, parents now have more time to spend with their children. Parents can not only gain a better appreciation of their schooling, but they can also become closer to their children socially and emotionally.

For those husbands and wives and other relationships whose jobs have made their personal interaction like ships passing in the night, the coronavirus present great opportunities to become closer. There are opportunities to have quality and meaningful conversations, share mutually enjoyable activities, and simply reconnect, get reacquainted, or get to know each other better.

What about self-renewal? Think about all those frustrating thoughts and times when you wished, yearned, for a chance to pursue a hobby, an intriguing interest, develop an exercise routine, read books, write a book, letters, essays—whatever is on your imagined or actual wish list. The coronavirus presents great opportunities to become closer to achieving some of those very things.

How can we apply our time, energy, and talents to help others in need as we practice social distancing? World leaders and elected officials have challenges, but so does each of us.

Yes, having to stay home because of business and school closures is no doubt causing financial and other kinds of hardship. But what can you do about it at this point? Fretting, worrying, and being irritable will not solve the problem. The best thing we all can do is make the most of it.

World leaders must make the most of this challenge. So, must we. As bad as it is, the coronavirus presents great opportunities to become closer in many areas of humanity.

Published March 25, 2020
htttps://janicesellis.com

DACA Exposes the Hypocrisy of Illegal Immigration

The Trump administration announced that it is rescinding the Deferred Action for Childhood Arrivals (DACA) executive action that the Obama administration put in place in 2012. The purpose of the action is for the children of illegal immigrants who entered the country as minors to receive a deferment from deportation and be eligible for a work permit.

Rescinding DACA exposes the hypocrisy of illegal immigration—an issue that United States Congress has failed or refused to deal with for decades. So, what does the rescinding DACA actually solve? The real issue is this country needs Immigration Reform Legislation.

On the cynical side, it is another Obama action that the Republicans seem hell bent on undoing. Also, it is Trump's way of pandering to the extremist wing of his base of supporters since he loudly and consistently promised that he would end DACA while on the campaign trail.

But how can targeting 800,000 young illegal immigrants—who came to the United States involuntarily, who are law-abiding, and hard-working—begin to solve the issue of what needs to be done with the twelve million immigrants that continue to live and work within our borders?

What is the point of threatening and creating anxiety and uncertainly among the small percentage of illegal immigrants who came forth and provided our government with all of their personal identification, trusting that they had the opportunity to ultimately become American citizens?

Rescinding DACA exposes the hypocrisy of the illegal immigration issue because lawmakers have not sought a permanent solution, which they have had ample opportunity to do so. Many lawmakers, for years, have refused to deal with the millions of illegal immigrants because of economic reasons.

It is common knowledge that illegal immigrants are a source of cheap labor. They support the agricultural industry and hold many domestic jobs from lawn care to house cleaning. Many companies knowingly hire illegal immigrants to avoid paying decent wages, avoid providing worker's benefits, and to avoid paying corporate taxes to the United States government.

So, who is fooled by this symbolic, hypocritical action by the Trump administration to rescind DACA?

And do you really expect Congress to have the courage and will to do in the next six months what it has been unwilling and unable to do in last two decades?

Rescinding DACA exposes the hypocrisy of illegal immigration—punishing a small segment of the most innocent among illegal immigrants, while ignoring the need to address millions more.

Are Americans that gullible?

Published September 6, 2017
https://janicesellis.com

Do You Approve of What Is Happening in Washington?

Do you approve of what is happening in Washington? Guess what? You have the power to change it. You really do. No, I am neither naïve, nor am I uninformed. What I do know is that too many of us have either given up, become cynical or disengaged.

We are our own worst enemy. We have chosen to accept defeat and let the powerful few make decisions, pass policies and legislation that is not in our best interest. We have abdicated our responsibility to hold those accountable whom we have voted for and elected to represent our interests, our beliefs, our values.

Worse yet, too many of us have decided not to vote at all and throw away our individual power. Let it simply be wasted. What is you answer when asked: Do you approve of what is happening in Washington? What steps are you taking to do something about it?

Elections have grave and lasting consequences. We see and hear about actions of elected officials playing out in the White House, in the halls of Congress every day. Many are not in the best interest of millions of American if not downright detrimental, whether it relates to health care, unequal access to education, justice, jobs.... You name it.

You can bring about needed changes through your vote. Change the decision makers. Change who you send to Washington to represent you.

Every vote counts. Every vote leads to victory for someone. If you vote for the wrong person or do not vote at all, you are still contributing to what goes on in your government at all levels. Imagine the President and members of Congress making decisions that are not in the best interest of most of the citizens or the country, and we just complain and sit by and do nothing.

Do you approve of what is happening in Washington? If not, what are you willing to do about it?

We all love to sit back, complain, point fingers, wring our hands, but our displeasure often stops there.

Nothing will change. Nothing will get better unless we combine our collective voices and our collective vote. We do that by each of us taking time to get involved

Published September 2018
https://janicesellis.com

New Alabama Immigration Law Begs for a National Solution

While some components of the new Immigration Law passed by the State of Alabama, if enacted, have troubling consequences, could it be the blueprint for the federal legislation that the President and Congress should pass?

No matter on what side of the immigration issue you find yourself, the solution will have losses and benefits for all involved. This is not a case of the good guys vs. the bad guys. The government, businesses, and the illegal immigrants share the blame in where we find ourselves today: More than eleven million undocumented immigrants live and work in the United States, with more slipping across our borders on a daily basis; many businesses, knowingly, employ them at lower wages to improve their profit margins; and the government is lax on enforcing laws already on the books to stem the tide.

Turning a blind eye, here and there, and doing business as usual with "eyes wide shut" is finally coming home to roost. The issue will not continually be ignored. The Alabama law all but guarantees it.

The Alabama law, if enforced, will finally get this issue out of the perpetual holding pattern it has been in for decades. The law covers most of the major issues that federal legislation needs to address.

The law—in addition to detaining immigrants who cannot produce proof of citizenship--penalizes any person, business, or institution that knowingly transports, hires, houses, or educates undocumented immigrants.

There are concerns about how this law will be carried out. Among them, law enforcement agencies can stop and detain someone they "suspect" of being in the country illegally until they produce proper documentation. In addition to the issue of racial profiling being a real concern, what will be done to those detainees who are here illegally? Imported? Deterred in some kind of make-shift prison or camp?

Another major concern is what about the children who have absolutely no say in the decision to come here illegally or to be born here to illegal parents? While they are currently getting a secondary education—but not able to go to college or apply competitively for a job. Now, these children may not be able to get an education at all.

Alabama is not the first state to take the matter into their own hands. First, there was Arizona, followed by Georgia, Utah, Indiana, and now Alabama. (The Supreme Court recently upheld the component of the Arizona law which penalizes businesses for knowingly hiring illegal immigrants.) What is to stop other states from accelerating passage of similar legislation?

But the Alabama law, the nation's toughest to date, screams that it is time for the President and Congress to deal with the immigration issue and pass major federal legislation.. With each state taking the issue into its own hands, there is the great potential of creating strife, divisiveness, human rights violations, and atrocities that are a throwback to chapters in our history that we would do well to keep closed.

What is the national policy for addressing the eleven million undocumented immigrants already living and working here? And what will be done to stop the influx of new one?

As harsh as the Alabama law may appear, it is a wake-up call to the federal government and to the nation that the issue can no longer be skirted.

The state of Alabama has decided how it will deal with illegal immigration. Will the Alabama law become the model?

Published June 19, 2012
USAonRace.com

Is Donald Trump a Role Model?

Is Donald Trump a role model, and if so, for what? Is he what Americans are looking for as their next President of the United States, the leader of the free world, and arguably the most visible and most powerful leader?

Does Trump represent the best among presidential candidates in both the Republican Party and Democratic Party?

So far, Donald Trump is long on sound bites and theatrics and short on civility and substance. What real leadership skills does he truly portray? Being president of the United States is not the same as being the star in his television show, *The Apprentice*. So far in this race, his behavior is demanding that America say in unison, "You are Fired."

How on earth can any rational, well-informed American take Trump seriously, using his own pronouncements, when it comes to the serious issues facing this country. Where are his realistic policies and plans to solve our long-standing immigration problem, to make America safer amid growing terrorism, to improve our education system so that our children will be better able to compete on the world stage in a global economy?

The only consistent thing Trump as advanced is how terrible things are and what a terrible job others are doing, and that we should support him because he will be great. Great at what?

Great at leveling personal insults at every opportunity at individuals and groups of people alike, great at proclaiming how all the people gathered at his political meetings and rallies love him, great at charging that everyone from the president on down is doing a terrible job at whatever job they hold. According to Trump no one or anything is working well in America.

Most proud Americans would consider most of his rhetoric and verbose speech very un-American.

America is far from perfect, but it is even farther from the negative, weak, and downtrodden picture that Donald Trump paints with his uncensored performances on and off the political trail.

Donald Trump as role model, for what and for whom? If you are ascribing to be someone who is great at grabbing the headlines no matter what you say, then Trump is your guy.

Published November 23, 2015
https://janicesellis.com

Are You in Favor of Passage of the DREAM Act?

The 2010 Census reveals that the Hispanic population is the largest minority population in the United States. The Hispanic population grew 43% between 2000—2010, while the African American population grew only 12.3% during the same period. Hispanics now make up 16.3% of the populations, while African Americans make up 12.6%.

The actual number of Hispanics living in the United States is even greater with the millions of illegal and undocumented immigrants.

During the past ten years, there have been attempt at the national and state level to pass the DREAM Act. DREAM is the acronym for Development, Relief and Education for Alien Minors.

The legislative proposal was originally introduced in the United States Senate in 2001. The most current legislation was introduced in March 2009 by U.S. Senator, Richard Durbin, and House of Representative Howard Berman. A Senate filibuster on December 18, 2010 blocked its passage at the national level. However, eleven states (Arkansas, California, Kansas, Maryland, Nebraska, New Mexico, Oklahoma, Texas, Utah, and Washington) have already passed legislation which would make undocumented immigrants eligible for in-state tuition benefits at a state's public colleges.

The description of the national DREAM Act legislation is as follows.

"The purpose of the Development, Relief and Education of Alien Minors, also called the DREAM Act, is to help those individuals who meet certain requirements have an opportunity to enlist in the military or go to college and have a path to citizenship which they otherwise would not have without this legislation. Supporters of the DREAM Act believe it is vital not only to the people who would benefit from it, but also the United States as a whole. It would give an opportunity to undocumented immigrant students who have been living in the U.S. since they were young, a chance to contribute back to the country that has given so much to them and a chance to utilize their hard-earned education and talents."

The national legislation furthers outlines a list of specific requirements needed to qualify for the benefits of the DREAM Act should it pass. Eligible undocumented immigrants must have:

- Entered the United States before the age of 16;

- Lived in the United States for at least five (5) consecutive years prior to the enactment of the bill;

- Graduated from a United States high school, or have

obtained a GED, or have been accepted into an institution of higher education (college/university);

- Good moral character; and

- Must be between the ages of 12 and 35 at the time of application

Should the DREAM Act pass at the national level, an undocumented individual meeting the requirements above, would also have to do a number of additional things to become apply and become a permanent U.S. citizen. Those addition conditions can be found at http://dreamact.info

If this legislation is re-introduced in the United States Congress this year or next year, should it pass and become law?

What do you think?

Published March 27, 2011
USAonRace.com

Playing to Racism: 2012 Presidential Candidates Missing a Great Opportunity

Whether it is Newt Gingrich calling President Obama the "Food Stamp President" or portraying poor black children as having only dope dealers for role models; or whether Ron Paul's racially inflammatory newsletters of ten years accurately defined his positions on race or not; or whether Rick Santorum's comments about blacks on welfare is paramount to them taking other citizens' money; or whether Rick Perry's N-word usage at the hunting "shack" on his property—whether these incidents depict the sentiment of the 21st Century Republican Party, what a missed, egregiously missed, opportunity!

What happened to the Republican Party of Abraham Lincoln? What happened to the Republican Party who was for abolitionism? What happen to the Republican Party of the Reconstruction Era after the Civil War?

Did you know that following the Civil War and during Reconstruction, blacks were very active in Republican Party politics and served in almost every level of government?

For more than a decade, blacks held offices from the United States Congress to state legislatures, city councils and county commissions. There were two senators and fourteen representatives in the US Congress alone. Blacks held more state offices in the Deep South than any place else. Blacks formed the majority in the House of Representatives for the state of South Carolina throughout that period—a state that gained recent notoriety for having fought vehemently to continue to fly the confederate flag atop its capitol.

Since Reconstruction, blacks have not had two US senators to serve in either party. And they certainly do not form a majority in any state's legislature. The reasons are subjects whose treatment could fill much more space than is available here. But the discussion is certainly worth having by civic-minded blacks and whites interested in making a two-party system work better for all groups irrespective of the outcomes of the November elections.

Does the Republican Party of the 21st Century not want blacks as members? Our two-party system of government will work at it best only when the participants represent the people not only in terms of political philosophy but also in ethnic, racial, and religious diversity.

Could it be that the recent alienation of black voters by the Republican Party candidates for President represents a definitive change in operative stereotypical views? That in fact they have regressed and bought the propaganda that all blacks are liberals. That all blacks believe in big government and prefer handouts over jobs and economic self-sufficiency?

Or is this sudden disinterest in the African American voter just a temporary suspension in judgment and a tactic to maximize the chance of maintaining a delicate balance of power in the state houses and Washington?

It will be a shame if leaders of the Republican Party wake up the morning or months after the November 2012 elections and realize their strategy of racial divisiveness was just a cruel hoax.

Irrespective of who ends up winning the 2012 elections, whether for President, members of Congress or local offices, minority groups, particularly African-Americans are in a great position to become more engaged in the two-party political process and make it work to address their interests. It is also a great opportunity for the Republican Party and black alike to dispel some harmful perceptions and labels.

One prevalent view is that most blacks are more liberal than conservative and therefore belong, or should belong, to the Democratic Party rather than the Republican Party. Along with that view are other philosophical assumptions that often come into play. On the individual level, there is a prevalent belief that most blacks believe in welfare and affirmative action programs rather than a good job and minimum taxes.

On the organizational level, there is the belief that the Democratic Party is more inclusive, empathetic, and supportive of the needs and interests of blacks than the Republican Party. While that may be case, the premise warrants frequent and close examination. What better time to examine those premises that during the 2012 Presidential Election?

Unfortunately, the Republican candidates for President of the United States have resorted to a strategy of racial polarization instead of racial inclusiveness.

Believe it or not, there are blacks who would love to embrace and be a part of a Republican Party that did not function on racial stereotypes and divisiveness, but the great individual rights and governing principles this wonderful country was founded upon.

So where is the disconnect? Is racism that blind?

Published January 27, 2012
USAonRace

During the 2012 Presidential Election, the Public Can Just Say "No"

It is time for the public to say "No." No, to the notion that we have become a society who would rather be entertained than informed as we go about the business of governing. No, to the sensationalism that has replaced rationalism in its power of influence when it comes to our collective decision-making process in selecting our leader.

Not to do so is to continue to allow the awesome power of the people, the public, to be minimized and debased. The stakes are much too high. The consequences are much too exacting.

During the upcoming elections, the public has a great opportunity to reclaim its rightful role in how political decisions and policies are made at the national, state, and local levels. We can and need to elevate our election process—imploring the noble within and around us, decrying and rejecting the base that tempts us.

To send a clear message and to stand our ground will be particularly important as we approach a presidential election that has the makings of being one of the most negative in recent history. Yet, the 2012 election will be one of the most important when it comes to the future direction of this country in terms of domestic and foreign policy.

Much, too much, is riding on who we select to lead the strongest nation in the free world.

One has only to look at the Republican primary debates, the mood, and actions in Congress to know that this could be one of the most negative elections in the country's history. Imagine months of distortions and misinformation.

But where does the blame lie?

If political action committees from major corporations and industries, labor unions and other special interest groups cannot spend their resources to disseminate factual information to educate and inform, then the public needs to recognize in whose best interest they are functioning and respond accordingly.

We, as a public, must send a resounding message to any candidate at any level that we cannot be duped, taken for granted, or misled. We are not interested, nor will we be tolerant of in any blood baths or extraneous side shows.

It is time for us to tune out and turn off messages that tug at our emotion rather than our sense of right and reason. It is time for us to hang-up on telephone calls from any camp where the truth is, at best, distorted and claims are not backed by facts.

Published December 16, 2011
USAonRace.com

Hillary Clinton or Donald Trump?

Hillary Clinton or Donald Trump for President of the United States? That is the ultimate question facing voters, and it is a critically important one.

But how can eligible voters, caring and concerned voters, arrive at the right decision not only for themselves, their families, but also the nation?

Cutting through the drama, the propaganda, the contradictions, and all manner of partisan politics makes it very difficult to find the truth. But one way to sort through this maze is to look at this as Clinton and Trump competing for the most important job in the world.

The job of president has major qualifications associated with it. There are certain skills, character traits, knowledge, and experience that the person who gets the job must have.

Do you know who best meets them, Hillary Clinton, or Donald Trump? As the clock winds down on this election, shouldn't that be the primary focus? Is Hillary Clinton or Donald Trump the most qualified to hold the office?

What are some of the most necessary qualifications? And can we make the tough decision, despite party affiliation or leaning, and truly say, "If the candidate doesn't meet these basics, can we really expect him or her to do the job?"

When considering whether the next president should be Hillary Clinton or Donald Trump, try to best determine who is the most knowledgeable and has consistently demonstrated that he or she has a command of the major issues, challenges and policies decisions facing the country. That knowledge should be in sufficient enough detail to distinguish between good advice and bad, to provide leadership and direction. In addition, he or she must have the communication, negotiation, and consensus-building skills to achieve meaningful outcomes.

Is it Hillary Clinton or Donald Trump who has the right and best kind of career experience to select the right cabinet or management team to grapple with some of the most complex issues facing our time within our borders and globally?

The President must be both an inclusive and compassionate leader if he or she is to balance the needs or the rich and the poor, the young and the elderly, the needs of minorities with those of the majority, the privileged and the disenfranchised in his or her decision-making. The President must perform the ultimate balancing act, making decisions based upon what is good for America and/or most Americans.

Strong integrity and high moral standards are also necessary qualifications for the job. When you sort through the facts and the partisan spin, who comes out with the edge on character and honesty, Hillary Clinton, or Donald Trump? A valuable clue is to look at what each has actually done during their careers and lifetime. And it is not the same – equally bad or equally good.

Hillary Clinton or Donald Trump? Given some needed qualifications, who is ready to do the job?

Published September 6, 2016
https://janicesellis.com

Living in the Moment Can Be Blinding

Living in the moment can be blinding and give us a distorted view of the past and put us on a wrong path for the future. This holds true in the 2016 United States Presidential Election.

The current Republican Presidential campaign is a great example of the danger of being caught in the reality TV-style tenor the whole process has taken. While it may be entertaining to watch, the underlying dangers are just beginning to manifest themselves.

Living in the moment can be blinding. History is replete with examples of how societies are destroyed from within because of the rise of what seems to be an attractive leader, at least for the moment, who in fact were Fascists, bigots, misogynists, and white supremacists.

Let us start with the front runner, Donald Trump. Many voters seem to be attracted to and captivated by his bold statements about anything from illegal immigrants, women, Muslims, Russia, China, Mexico, and opposing candidates. It seems not to matter whether those statements are false, contradictory, vulgar, or incite hate or violent behavior. In Trump's case words seem not to matter beyond the moment.

His rise to front runner status among Republican candidates for president is a great example of how living in the moment can be blinding. And when you open your eyes, it may be too late.

With Trump continuously repeating insults to Mexican Americans, legal and illegal immigrants alike; with Trump continuously insulting all Muslims, even those who do not support terrorists or extremists; with his frequent insults of women as exemplified by his treatment of Fox News journalist, Megan Kelly, how can his supporters possible think that even if he wins the Republican nomination that he can get Hispanics, blacks, Muslims, and other minorities in the electorate to vote for him?

Will Trump be able to attract a large enough percentage of the largest voting group, women, to win? These are real questions. Living in the moment can be blinding and prevent realistic analysis of some likely answers.

Will a Donald Trump presidency be good for the country? Will he actually be able to do what he says should he get elected? Living in the moment can be blinding and potentially dangerous when we consider the great stakes riding on the outcome of the 2016 Presidential Election.

We must remain mindful that living in the moment can be blinding, resulting in dire consequences for our country, our community, and our family unit.

Published March 20, 2016
https://janicesellis.com

Donald Trump As Role Model

Donald Trump as role model for whom and for what. Is he what Americans are looking for as their next President of the United States, the leader of the free world, and arguably the most visible and most powerful leader?

Does Trump represent the best among presidential candidates in both the Republican Party and Democratic Party?

So far, Donald Trump is long on sound bites and theatrics and short on civility and substance.

His recent mocking of a disabled reporter who works for *The New York Times* newspaper is just the latest among many instances of outrageous behavior.

Donald Trump as role model.

What real leadership skills does he truly portray? Being president of the United States is not the same as being the star in his television show, *The Apprentice*. So far in this race, his behavior is demanding that the majority of American voters say, "You are fired."

How on earth can any rational, well-informed American voter take Trump seriously, using his own pronouncements, when it comes to the serious issues facing this country? Where are his realistic policies and plans to solve our long-standing immigration problem, to make America safer amid growing terrorism, to improve our education system so that our children will be better able to compete on the world stage in a global economy?

The only consistent thing Trump has advanced is how terrible things are and what a terrible job others are doing, and that we should support him because he will be so great. Great at what?

Great at leveling personal insults at every opportunity at individuals and groups of people, alike. Great at proclaiming how all the people gathered at his political meetings and rallies love him. Great at charging that everyone from the president on down is doing a terrible job at whatever job they hold.

Donald Trump as role model. Does his speech and behavior represent what most Americans are all about?

According to Trump no one or anything is working well in America. Most proud Americans would consider most of his rhetoric and verbose speech very un-American.

America is far from perfect, but it is even farther from the negative, weak, and downtrodden picture that Donald Trump paints with his uncensored performances on and off the political trail.

Donald Trump as role model, for what and for whom? If you are ascribing to be someone who is great at grabbing the headlines no matter what you say, then Trump is your guy.

Published November 27, 2015
https://janicesellis.com

Elected Officials Work for You

Right now, we need to ask in these tough times, are our elected officials working for our best interest. When you look at some of their decisions for our families and children, at a minimum, it leaves you scratching your head.

The Missouri Legislature will end its regular session today. They have forwarded a budget to the Governor that significantly cuts K-12 education when our children are already struggling to make the grade in crowded classroom, with many teachers who need additional resources to effectively educate them.

This budget will put an additional burden on poor working families to get adequate health care by reducing dollars for Medicaid, totally eliminating state health insurance for some children (MC+ for Kids), and charging a fee (Co-Pay) for others whose parents are barely making enough money to make ends meet.

There is a foster care bill that has provisions which put foster care children even more at risk while the system remains understaffed and underfunded.

Why do many of our elected officials think these decisions are acceptable? Why should those who can least afford it continue to bare a disproportionate share of the burden to balance the state budget? We can raise revenues and pass policies to get downtown renovated, building built, but we cannot find the dollars for education and healthcare services?

Elected officials work for the people. Our tax dollars pay their salaries. They are accountable to us. If they are not doing what we need them to do on our behalf, we need to seriously ask, why not? More importantly, why do we continually let them get away with it? Just think about it.

Would you put someone in a job and never check to see how well he or she is performing? After listening to job seekers rail about their qualifications and experience, and how they are best for the job, would you hire them and forget them, leaving them to their own devices? Hardly. Especially if it were your company or you were paying them with your hard-earned money.

But, as citizens, isn't that exactly what most of us do after voting and working for—essentially hiring—elected officials? After the promises, the vote, or non-vote, the election night victory parties, we often retire and relinquish our roles in ensuring that our government works for us.

As you watch the decisions on the national, state, and local levels, how are they improving the quality of your family's life, your community, your employment, and career opportunities? We would do well to ask: "Are we better off today than we were two years ago?" We can also shout the familiar refrain: "It's the economy stupid."

USING MY WORD POWER

Another election is upon us. President Bush and many Senators, Representatives will be out campaigning for election 2004. But this election could hardly be characterized as the usual state of affairs for all the reasons we have lived through: 911, the war with Iraq, a growing deficit, a bulging national debt, and a never-ending war on terrorism.

But that is only part of it. Is anyone factoring in the crises we face on the home front. The unemployment ranks grow daily. We still are not making the grade when it comes to providing a quality education for all of our children. We still have far too high a rate of drug, alcohol and substance abuse plaguing our communities. We still have too many children put in harm's way because they do not have quality and safe programs after school.

So, when we do not see a lot of change in sight, what can be expected? Hardly, the usual fare. The public is bound to see their government at work, or not at work, in ways it has not seen before.

But will we, the public, fall into our usual role of absent employer, never bothering to proactively check on what is being done by those we hired in fulfilling their promises to make life better on our behalf? At best, will we fall into our role as passive spectator, complaining but never bothering to make a call, write a letter, or convene a meeting of like-minded citizens to hold elected officials accountable?

If we do not watch out for what is in our best interest, we cannot expect anyone else to do so either.

There is much to be involved in and vigilant about—from where our children go to school, what money is left from our paycheck to improve our standard of living, to the quality and bacteria-free food we put on our tables for our loved ones to eat. If you just stop to think about it, decisions made by elected and appointed officials every day at every level of government is eventually felt in our daily lives. There are few or no exceptions.

The vigilance and involvement begin at home with your local elected officials and spread to the state and national level. Their performance is interconnected.

Work requirements among elected and appointed officials are no different than many of those you and I are required to meet: 1) an obligation to know your job and carry it out in a manner that will make things better, not worse; and 2) the need to be a team player, pulling together to get the best outcome. So, should we expect any less from those that we have hired to govern?

What will you do to not hold elected officials—both new and veteran—accountable for the very important jobs they are expected to carry out?

There is too much riding on it—for our families, for our community.

Published May 16, 2003
The Kansas City Call

Electing Best Leaders for Times Ahead

The upcoming elections in November, unlike many others, should not be treated as your ordinary, off-year, marginally obligatory, civic affair. The outcomes of too many important issues are riding on who we choose to represent us.

We can ill afford to be disinterested and disengaged. The healthcare reform issue has shown us that. But there are critical issues beyond healthcare reform.

On the international front, we are in an atypical and interminable war or terrorism. We seem obliged to continue to engage in traditional military combat in Afghanistan where we have put thousands of our sons and daughters in harm's way. We are ever watchful of other hot beds of instability that could threaten our well-being: Iran, Yemen, and Iraq—still. Right here at home, we have seen and unseen terrorists in our midst.

On the domestic front, many issues abound. We are in the midst of one of the worst economic conditions in recent history—a deep depression that is reminiscent of the Great Depression. Unemployment is unacceptably high, which has a ripple effect in so many ways.

Despite the financial meltdown on Wall Street that required government bailouts to prevent us from slipping into an economic catastrophe that would have rivaled the Great Depression, we still have uncontrolled greed on the part of executives in some of the nation's largest and most prestigious corporations and investment houses on Wall Street. This dichotomy still severely hurts and undermined consumers' confidence in the fundamentals of our economy.

As if the protracted war on terrorism at home and abroad, and a fledgling economy were not enough, there are other issues coming home to roost. Our complacency with an educational system that fails too many children can no longer be ignored. If we do not take seriously the mantra, "Leave no child behind," some crazed terrorist will be the least of our concerns or fears in the long run. The quality education deficit is both a national and international issue, threatening our long-term well-being and our place on the global stage.

While a recent bill on healthcare reform was passed, it highlighted how dysfunctional the political process can be when elected officials put their own selfish interest ahead of those of the people who elected them.

This is not a Presidential election year, but it is a critically important election year. As a voter that can shape the outcome, are you engaged? Are you bothering to see where candidates stand on the major issues we face as a nation, as a local community. War, the economy, education are issues that connect us all.

While we love waving the flag in reverie about this republic of ours, we have a less than illustrious record of participating in how it is governed. Our voting record in Presidential elections is nothing to write to a new democracy about. But our voting pattern in non-Presidential, alias off-year, elections is so abysmal that it should be used as an example of how the democratic process can be rendered impotent.

Most pundits are predicting that this November election will be a dramatic one because of all the partisan contention around the passage of health care reform legislation. Granted it has shown the democratic process at its ugliest—not only in the halls of Congress but in the streets across America. From shout outs of disrespect in the Congressional Chamber to the shouting of racial epithets on the sidewalks.

Must our voracious appetite for the dramatic be whetted to get our attention, to engage us, to motivate us to act? Does that explain why we will bother some of the time to go out and vote for a presidential candidate, yet never go out to vote for a Congressional candidate, state legislator, or a needed referendum?

Do we not believe in the words and wisdom of one of the nation's most tenured and most effective Congressmen, the late Tip O'Neal, that "All politics is local." Whether it is fixing roads or fixing schools, it really starts and stops right in the voting booth with our selections of who we send to the state houses and Washington.

That being said, which candidate in the respective offices will best handle the issues that are important to you, your family, your community, your state?

War, education, healthcare, corporate corruption, the economy, better roads, tax reform, the environment. If one or more of these issues, or some other, is of concern to you, one thing is certain: Whoever is elected, with or without your involvement, will have the power to make these issues better or worse. You can also be certain that the quality of your life will be affected one way or the other.

Published May 5, 2010
USAonRace.com

Continual Erosion of Profile of Political Leaders

If you were asked to profile a contemporary elected official, what would that profile look like? When we look at the pervasiveness of alleged, and substantiated, immoral, unethical, and illegal behavior among many of our elected and appointed officials, we would likely find it painful when that profile is placed up against reality vs. the attainable. It would be even more painful to compare a realistic profile to the ideal.

In recent years, we seemed besieged by intermittent revelations of scandal. Most recently the incidents range from murder charges against the mayor of York, New Jersey, to two of our US Senators currently under federal investigation, one for gross campaign finance violations, the other for money laundering and ties to organized crime. The claims of corruption, unethical or illegal behavior, and other miscarriages of justice seem never ending.

And you thought the parade of political perversity would end with the Clinton Administration. There was hope that the country would be in for a period of reprieve.

With the emerging scandal involving California Congressman Gary Condit, and the un-abating negative perception of politics and politicians, a reprieve seems not to be in sight. And if it were not Congressman Condit, would it be someone else? That certainly could be a growing public sentiment.

What messages are such episodes sending the leaders of tomorrow? Are they being turned off by what they see? Or are they, hopefully, realizing how in need our government is, at all levels, for men and women who have strong values, and good character?

Let us all hope that the latter is true. Let us hope that this latest and entirely shameful, irresponsible behavior or the part of Congressman Condit, and many before him, will not leave our pool of political talent bankrupt because of growing disgust about many of our political leaders.

Many people believe that either most politicians are corrupt or corruptible. Many believe that the promises and the word of politicians are only good until a better deal comes along. Many people believe that the average politician is only committed to doing whatever it takes to win the next election, and they will sell their soul, or what's left of it, to stay elected.

Even if those traits do not describe most politicians, the behavior of many politicians does little to dispel the notions. Congressman Condit' behavior as it related to missing intern Chandra Levy certainly does not help his image and it further damages, unfortunately, the credibility of fellow elected officials. Not only does he join a host of elected official who have had or admitted to having extramarital affairs, he too, like many of them chose to be dishonest about.

Tragically, the intern with whom he has admitted having an affair is also missing. What are his constituents to think? What are we, as concerned citizens, to think?

Through this seemingly trough of negativity dominating the political stage at many levels, we must not allow it to do lasting harm.

We need to proactively engage in a conversation with our children—future leaders—about our political leaders, albeit they are imperfect. We must note that the institutions of government are stronger than any one person or one group of persons. We can remind our children of a country that has withstood the ruins of war, the ugliness and divisiveness of slavery. It has withstood a great depression, many economic recessions, and other crises of various sizes. Each of these events and episodes had both honorable and not-so-honorable leaders on the stage, those who had strong character and functioned with the highest integrity, and those who were morally weak and ethically challenged.

Like those seminal events in our history, the country is still strong enough to withstand what is turning out to be a protracted period of tarnished leadership—leadership seemingly devoid of high moral, ethical standards, and intrepid integrity.

We must hold those political leaders of high moral conviction and character out as examples in our conversations around the dinner table, the fireplace, and in the family room.

With one scandal or another involving our leaders all too often dominating the news, is it any wonder that it is becoming more and more difficult to keep the public from being continuously drawn in the cesspool of cynicism?

How can we prevent our young, future leaders from falling in?

Published July 10, 2001
The Kansas City Star

GOP Wooing Black Voter—Courtship or Marriage?

Our two-party system of government will work at its best only when the participants represent the people not only in terms of political philosophy but also in ethnic, racial, and religious diversity.

Could it be that the recent local and national attention that the Republican Party is giving black voters represents a definitive change in operative stereotypical views? That in fact there is a realization that all blacks are not liberals. That all blacks do not believe in big government and prefer handouts over economic self-sufficiency.

Or is this sudden interest in the African American voter just a temporary suspension in judgment and a tactic to maximize the chance of maintaining a delicate balance of power in the state houses and Washington?

It will be a shame if one wakes up one morning months after the November elections and realizes it was just a cruel courtship hoax—woo them, catch them, use them to satisfy an immediate need, and then return to political business as usual.

Courting the black voter has become a high-stake game in Missouri, especially in the U.S. Senate race between

Democratic candidate Jean Carnahan, and Republican candidate Jim Talent. Both parties acknowledge that the level of turnout among the state's African-American voters can determine who wins the Senate seat. This Senate seat could also determine the balance of power in the U.S. Senate.

It appears that the GOP and candidate Jim Talent are going all out to woo the black voters in Missouri. One has only to listen to the GOP radio ads attacking the records and actions of Democratic leaders from a county executive, a mayor, the Governor to the House Minority Leader of the US House of Representatives.

Irrespective of who ends up winning the seat in the Missouri US Senate race as well as races all across the state, minority groups, particularly African-Americans are in a great position to become very engaged in the two-party political process and make it work to address their interests. It is also a great opportunity to dispel some harmful perceptions and labels.

One prevalent view is that most blacks are more liberal than conservative and therefore belong, or should belong, to the Democratic Party rather than the Republican Party. Along with that view are other philosophical assumptions that often come into play. On the individual level, there is a prevalent belief that most blacks believe in welfare and affirmative action programs rather than a good job and minimum taxes.

On the organizational level, there is the belief that the Democratic Party is more inclusive, empathetic, and supportive of the needs and interests of blacks than the Republican Party. While that may be case, the premise warrants frequent and close examination.

Among ardent die-hard Democrats and Republicans alike, these stereotypical notions could stir heated debate in many circles. But past and recent history could provide interesting facts to engage the discussion.

For example, does the appointment of African-Americans in important positions in the Bush administration represent a genuine effort of inclusiveness? Is it a clue to how the Republican Party will move forward in the future, perhaps reaching back and taking lessons from its own history?

Did you know that following the Civil War and during Reconstruction, blacks were very active in Republican Party politics and served in almost every level of government?

For more than a decade, blacks held offices from the United States Congress to state legislatures, city councils and county commissions. There were two senators and fourteen representatives in the US Congress alone. Blacks held more state offices in the Deep South than any place else. Blacks formed the majority in the House of Representatives for the state of South Carolina throughout that period--a state that gained recent notoriety for having fought vehemently to continue to fly the confederate flag atop its capitol.

Since Reconstruction, blacks have not had two US senators to serve in either party. And they certainly do not form a majority in any state's legislature. The reasons are subjects whose treatment could fill much more space than is available here. But, the discussion is certainly worth having by civic-minded blacks and whites interested in making a two party system work better for all groups irrespective of the outcomes of the November elections.

If one party's philosophy or interests are not representing or benefiting you and your community, how can you ever hope to change it if you are not sitting around the table in meaningful discussion and arguing the case?

What good is it to have your interests looked after for four years only to be ignored, if not totally diminished, the next four years? Furthermore, how can you fight for what is in the best interest of your state, your city, your community, your family if you are absent?

We have a two-party system of government in this country. One or the other will always be in a position to call the shots about your quality of life. You should make it your business to have a say no matter which party is in power.

The real question today is: Will African American voters take advantage of this newfound interest of the Republican Party and use it to address the educational, economic, and other needs to gain notable and long-lasting positions at the political power-brokering table? It could be a significant step in the right direction.

Published October 11, 2002
The Kansas City Star

Government Is Big Business: What Has Been Your Experience Lately?

With the 2012 Presidential Election in full campaign mode, the central theme among candidates is jobs and what and how the next president should get more Americans back to work—what should be done to get the economy healthy again.

What about the perennial issue of how government functions, period?

Government is big business. Some would argue that it is among our biggest businesses—not only in Washington, but in local and regional offices across the nation, and its satellite offices (embassies, military bases) around the world. But many of us rarely think of government in that light because of the bureaucracy and the apparent inefficiency and slowness in which things seem to get done.

Government often becomes the "whipping boy" for the private sector even when improvements have been implemented over the years. Government has a branding problem. It is in need of an image makeover. Even the good and efficient branches are being tainted by their less-efficient and less-effective counterparts.

There are many lessons and practices that can be learned from a well-run business and corporate environment that will serve governmental agencies, bureaus, and departments well. Bringing business concepts such as "customer service" and "user friendly" from the private sector and applying them to the public sector could be a basic start.

While one could list a number of things that have contributed to the low esteem in which many businesses and tax paying citizens hold government and its employees, top of the list is the difficulty John or Jane Q. Citizen has in simply getting a question answered and a problem addressed in a timely manner. It is not uncommon to call some governmental agency, at the city, state, or federal level in search of information that you would think would be at one's fingertips, only to find that the person answering the phone hasn't a clue as to what you are talking about.

To add insult to injury, the person answering the phone might boldly indicate that he or she is not the least bit interested in trying to find out what you are talking about or how he or she might assist you in solving your problem. And God forbid, if you are persistent, and point blank ask them if they could bother to provide further assistance. In addition to the obvious irritation in their voice, you might get any number of reasons or excuses as to why they are unable or simply will not be of much assistance.

With such an experience, you, as businessperson or a taxpayer, are left with a bad sound in your ear, and not a very good feeling about the governmental entity from which you are seeking assistance or just information. Furthermore, you hang up the phone or walk away shaking your head and saying to yourself, such behavior would not be tolerated very long if you received such treatment from someone who worked in a department store. If you did not get any satisfaction when you complained to the store manager, you would gladly take your business elsewhere.

However, taking our business elsewhere is not an option when we fail to get good service from a city, county, state, or any other governmental agency employee. Too often, we are simply left with a bad image in our minds which colors our view of government and how business is run within its walls—inefficiently by inefficient, non-caring, protected employees.

Taking a proactive stand to apply competitive principles and practices in the management and delivery of public services could be a very good thing for both city employees and the citizenry alike. Many cities have moved or are moving to privatization of certain services. They are actually looking to the private sector to see if certain services can be provided in a high quality, timely and more cost-effective manner which not only improves operations, but also makes citizens happier, thereby improving the image and relationship all the way around.

Many cities fear privatization of services. Perhaps, a city need not resort to privatization of services if it would focus on basic marketing principles. How about marketization of services?

Marketization of services means that governmental departments and agencies create an environment where creativity and competition to deliver services better and more efficiently is not only encouraged, but also required. *Encourage* and *reward* the kind of work performance among governmental employees and departments that engenders pride that lets them know they are second to none in carrying out the duties and responsibilities of their jobs. That, indeed, when compared to private sector performance, they measure up.

Striving for good customer service, making it easy for citizens to get basic information about their government, get a simple problem solved i.e., creating a user-friendly environment, could go a long way in reversing the poor image many citizens hold of their elected and paid public servants.

After all, John and Jane Q Citizen are paying customers, too. They deserve the best in customer service.

Marketization of government services--applying private business practices to the public sector. It needs to happen more and more irrespective of who becomes our next president, governor, or mayor.

Published January 20, 2012
https://janicesellis.com

Growing Protest Against Trump

Growing protest against Trump, what does it mean? Are caring citizens finally waking up or are the demonstrations orchestrated by the anti-Trump establishment?

Whatever the reasons or whomever is behind them, the protests signal that there is growing concern that Donald Trump has a great chance of being the Republican nominee for President of the United States. That also means that there is a good chance he could become the 45th President of the United States.

Growing protest against Trump at least is an expression of disapproval and growing unpopularity of the provocative statements and policies that have and are defining the Trump candidacy. Trumps has shown no reluctance in insulting and deriding entire groups of people. It has not been confined to illegal immigrants, the target he used to kick off his campaign. At that time, he declared that they were "rapists and murderers."

Building a wall on the Mexico-U.S. border to keep them out of America has been a constant refrain. Deporting illegal immigrants currently living here remains his top priority. In addition to Hispanics participating in the protests, those who are here and eligible to vote are registering in record numbers to vote in the November election.

Does the growing protest against Trump include more than Hispanics? Are there caring citizens who are finally realizing the possible national and global consequences of a Trump presidency?

Could it be that sensible, logical, intelligent, and thinking American voters are finally saying?

"What do Trump statements and pronouncements really mean? Where are the details? What do they mean for the country at home and on the world stage"?

More importantly, what will it say about America if a candidate like Trump, who make false and contradictory statements within the same day, sometime within the same hour; who consistently shows a lack of understanding of how the three branches of government supposed to work; who shows a lack of knowledge of history or foreign policy. How can he possibly be the leader of the free world?

Could the growing protest against Trump possibly mean that caring American voters are finally listening and paying attention?

Published March 21, 2016
https://janicesellis.com

Adequate Health Care Coverage: Too Many Americans Do Not Have It

Amid the clamor on the Presidential campaign trail to repeal the HealthCare Bill passed by President Barack Obama, one has yet to hear what will be put in its place. Access to adequate health insurance coverage is still out of reach for many Americans—over 47 million. That number likely climbs daily with the persistent unemployment rate.

Even before we entered the current recession, pockets of poverty seem to be an insidious part of the economic landscape. The faces of poverty seem not to have changed over that same period of time. And too often, a lack of adequate health care coverage is one of the constant companions of poverty.

Of course, poverty and a lack of adequate health care coverage results in poor health—poor health because families cannot afford to practice prevention and take care of minor problems before that turn in to major ones.

And who make up the country's poor and uninsured? Blacks, Hispanics, low-income whites, and their children are among the poorest groups in the nation.

All of these people are not on welfare. Many work two jobs to make ends meet. The problem is that many have jobs that do not offer health insurance as a benefit. So, the hard worker not only works hard but also cannot afford a day off if he/she becomes sick. So often, acute, and minor health problems turn into chronic and catastrophic diseases.

Imagine the consequences—long and short-term on our children. Among the many challenges poorer children face every day, imagine them performing at their best in school when they are not feeling well, and their parents cannot afford a doctor's visit or the medications to knock out a common childhood infection or illness.

While we are in a serious economic slump, America is still one of the richest nations on earth. It begs the question why so many Americans lack adequate health care coverage? And why do we as a society continue to fail at finding solutions to stem the tide? President Obama is trying with the passage of his Health Care bill. But partisan opposition rather than improve it or make any necessary changes, they would rather make it a political punching bag.

What then should be put in place? Instead of reducing the number of uninsured, and those with inadequate health care coverage, "Obama Care" (as is negatively characterized) if repealed will certainly result in more people being left outside the healthcare system.

Yes, there are government programs, and some private initiatives, to help those in need. But none seems to solve the revolving door of poor health care coverage for so many Americans.

The problem is a very complex one, and so is the solution.

But making a concerted effort to reduce the number of uninsured and underinsured should be a part of the legislative agenda at all levels of government. And while candidates are seeking your vote in the upcoming Presidential elections, we need to ask them if not "Obama Care" then what?

Listen carefully to their answers. What is their plan for making health care coverage available for forty-seven million Americans?

What is their solution?

Published February 2, 2012
USAonRace.com

Outcomes of 2020 Elections Will Be Critical

The political campaign season is well on the way. The outcomes of 2020 elections will be critical in determining the future of America. Who we elect for President, and who we elect to represent us in the US Senate and House of Representatives should be of ultimate concern.

It is not too early to begin evaluating President Trump and every candidate vying to be the Democratic Nominee to run against him. You have an opportunity to help determine who will be the next President of the United States.

You may be wondering what specifically can be done that would make a difference. There is a lot you can do. First, take some time to list the issues that are most important to you, your family, your community, and your country. It is your country as much as it is anyone else.

Consider each of those areas very carefully. Which candidate are concerned about the same issues? How are they prioritize in his/her platform? Outcomes of 2020 elections will be critical.

Focus on those issues that the President, Senators and Representatives can do something about if they have the will to do so. Issues like making sure Americans have access to quality health care, access to a quality education, jobs with livable wages, affordable housing, improved race relations, immigration policy, the environment, etc.

A candidate saying what you might want to hear is not enough. All of the candidates have a record. Take a little time and find out how they have voted on issues that you care about. Find out what they have achieved during their terms in office.

Nothing is more important than each citizen fulfilling their responsibility to ensure that our democratic form of government works and remains strong. Who you elect will have a direct effect on the quality of your life. What is done is Washington is felt in households and communities all across America.

Each of us much go through the same process when we choose a local elected officials. Do they share our values and priorities? Whether voting at the national or local level, the outcomes of 2020 elections will be critical.

Published June 27, 2019
https://janicesellis.com

Donald Trump Continues to Question President Obama's Place of Birth

It is 2012, and Donald Trump continues to question the place of President Barack Obama's place of birth.

Is it in the name? Is it the belief by more than 25% of Americans that he is Muslim despite his repeated affirmation that he is Christian, and doubt that he was born in the United States? Or is it because he is the first black President of the United States?

Unlike any other president before him, President Barack Obama's place of birth is persistently challenged. It began when he won the Democratic Primaries in 2008. The claims have been made by Republican elected officials, many fringe activists, and prospective political opponents. The latest to join the ranks of the "Birthers" is none other than the renowned businessman, Donald Trump, who has also announced that he is considering running for president of the United States himself—against President Obama.

Republican members of Congress and state legislatures have proposed and voted for legislation that would require presidential candidates to provide documentation of their qualifications to be president, including natural-born citizenship.

Lawsuits have been filed in lower courts, seeking to disqualify Obama as President. They have all been rejected by the lower courts. Three lawsuits have gone all the way to the United States Supreme Court but have also been dismissed.

Despite the state of Hawaii releasing an official birth record, the newspaper announcement of birth submitted by the hospital where President Obama was born, and the findings of investigative reports of journalists from around the world who confirm that he was indeed born in the United States, there are those who continue to persist that he was not.

Why?

Has any other president been asked to produce a birth certificate to prove that he is a natural citizen of the United States?

Why isn't President Obama birth certificate proof enough?

In terms of his religious faith, why are there media and political leaders who still proffer over the airways that President Obama is Muslim? Is it the negative "cloud" of being a sympathizer and practitioner of terrorism that is associated with the religion that is driving the conspiracy theorists? Is it because Obama doesn't wear his religious faith on his sleeve and is not seen worshiping every Sunday at a Church in Washington, D.C.?

Did people question President Ronald Reagan and other presidents who were not seen going to church on Sundays? Do we even know the religious affiliation of all of our past presidents?

We certainly have never questioned where they were born, or their religious beliefs, and question it so doggedly.

Specifically: Why do you think the birthplace and religion of President Barack Obama continues to be challenged? What more do you think President Obama should do, if he can do anything, once and for all to quell the accusations?

Published June 1, 2012
https://janicesellis.com

Political Leaders of Tomorrow

To the political leaders of tomorrow, what impressions are we leaving today? With the gridlock in Washington, and the pervasive negative perception of politics and politicians, what messages are we sending the leaders of tomorrow? Are they being turned off by what they see?

Or are they, hopefully, realizing how in need our government is, at all levels, for good men and women? Men and women who have strong values, good character, and a true desire to devote their talent and energy toward those area that impact public policy and people's lives.

Let us all hope that the latter is true, and that the entire shameful, irresponsible behavior of many elected officials will not leave our pool of political talent bankrupt. Politics, and the political process is much too important, to suffer permanent injury.

Whether we like the people elected, the rules or the processes outlined in the Constitution of the United States, they impact every aspect of our lives. Politics, public policy, and the people we elect determines many things about the quality of our lives, from where we live to how we live. Through this seemingly unending negativity dominating the political stage on all levels, we must not let our future leaders be left with a negative view or bad taste in their mouths about government and how it works. We need to emphasize that this too shall pass.

We must remind them on every turn about the great system of government that we have in this country, albeit imperfect. We must note that the institution is stronger than any one person or one group of persons. The country has withstood the ugliness and divisiveness of slavery. It has withstood wars. It has withstood a depression, many economic recessions, and other crises of various sizes. The country is strong enough to withstand what looks like this period of unbreakable gridlock.

Including our government and effective political leaders in our conversations around the dinner table, the fireplace, and in the family room will go a long way to instill a sense of what good public service is all about. Openly discuss political events with the young impressionable minds around us. Encourage a conversation where issues will be aired and put into the proper perspective—helping people to resolve conflicting feelings that may make them avoid public life.

In our classrooms, at every opportunity, we need to be looking to the great philosophers and leaders in classic and recent history for guidance and as examples to follow. Leaders, who are morally and ethically strong, providing leadership in upholding what is good about America, still represent the heart and soul of politics.

Politics still mean those deliberations, active, sometimes vigorous, and lively discussions, among citizens who diligently searched to determine and promote the greatest good for the greatest number with each policy decision made.

For this to continue to be a great country, it will take us all to remain engaged, participating at all levels in whatever way we can to keep our government strong.

Now is the time to voice our feelings and positions in record numbers. It is not the time to succumb to our feeling or disappointment and disgust.

Let us send a resounding message to our leaders of tomorrow that politics, the political stage, and all of its imperfections, are an integral and inextricable part of our lives. We cannot cut it out. Our apathy or disenchantment with it will not make it go away.

Perhaps the greatest message we can send to the leaders of tomorrow is to vote in record numbers in local and national elections.

Show them that you still care about your government.

Published November 21, 22014
https://janicesellis.com

President Trump Is Promoting Blatant Racism As the New Normal

Whether it is a policy initiative or a crude outburst, President Trump is promoting blatant racism as the new normal in America. While some of us may be appalled at what he says and does, we should be more alarmed at the millions of Americans that agree with him. His so-called base and other in-the-closet supporters.

The most frightening thing is that there are millions of Americans—neighbors, colleagues, family members, policy makers, business leaders—who not only find nothing wrong with what he says and does, but agree with him, defend them. And, worse of all, they urge him on, giving him carte blanche, comfort and encouragement to keep spewing racial divisiveness, hatred, and all manner of baseness.

What can we do to reclaim our country, our dignity, our humanity before it is too late? How much more are we willing to tolerate? How much more are we willing to excuse? How much more are we to overlook and say, "Oh, that is Trump being Trump?" President Trump is promoting blatant racism as the new normal. But only a few leaders, Republican or Democrats, are expressing outrage. And where are the decent and caring Americans?

Donald Trump is not the problem. WE are. We are the ones who are watching and accepting behavior that is anything other than Presidential. Behavior that is anything other than is in the best interest of America. Behavior that is anything other than that, which shows America as an honorable and rational leader of the free world. Even worse, it is behavior that is riddled with untruths and no regard for the history and principles on which the country was built.

The world is watching and must be wondering what will it take for Americans to say, ENOUGH? President Trump is promoting blatant racism as the new normal, and most of us are content with just expressing outrage.

The latest degrading commentary about immigrants from Africa, Haiti, and other countries of color not only shows deep-seated racism, but total ignorance and a disregard of history. People of color were in America before other immigrants arrived. People of color have helped build and made American what it is today. He and his supporters may be the only ones who will try to change and ignore those facts.

What is it about history and truth that President Trump and his followers and enablers do not get? If we are not careful we will become numb and silent participants in this terrible agenda where President Trump is promoting blatant racism as the new normal.

Imagine what kind of America we will have, what life will be like for all Americans, when blatant and ugly racist dialogue and behavior are acceptable, normal occurrences.

Is this what our children and future generations have to look forward to? Shame on US.

Published January 17, 2018
https://janicesellis.com

Qualifications to Be President of United States

What are the qualifications to be President of United States? Now is the time to ask that question as you prepare to cast a vote in the 2020 election.

What qualifications do you think the president should have for what is arguably the number one job in the world? More importantly, among the candidates vying for the job, who best meets them?

Who is best to uphold America's form of government and the good values that set it apart from most nations in the world?

These are the overriding question for the 2020 Presidential Election. America is not perfect, and the President's focus should be to make it better.

First and foremost, the president should know this country's history, the role, structure, and function of our form government. The president should be the role model when it comes to respecting and upholding the Constitution and the rule of law.

Which candidate consistently demonstrates a command of the major issues, challenges and policies decisions facing the country in sufficient enough detail to distinguish between good advice and bad, to provide leadership and direction, and has the communication, negotiation, and consensus-building skills to achieve meaningful outcomes?

For such an important position, who we choose must have the right experience. He or she must be able to select the right cabinet or management team to grapple with some of the most complex issues facing our time within our borders and globally.

What is their vision for the country? Is it realistic and achievable?

The President must be both inclusive and compassionate to balance the needs or the rich and the poor, the young and the elderly, the needs of minorities with those of the majority, the privileged and the disenfranchised. The President must perform the ultimate balancing act, making decisions based upon what is good for America and/or most Americans.

By the time we cast our vote if we have not determined which candidate has strong integrity, high moral standards, is a unifier and not a divider, then same on us.

These are the minimum qualifications to be president of United States. Who best meets them?

Published July 29, 2019
https://janicesellis.com

Impeachment Trial Is to Protect the Country

Whether a supporter or opponent of President Donald J. Trump, the impeachment trial is to protect the country. It is hoped that every American citizen believes that senators should conduct a fair trial in determining whether impeachable crimes have been committed against the country.

No matter whether a member of the Republican Party or Democratic Party, United States Senators' first obligation in an impeachment trial is to protect the country. Senators take an oath to support and uphold the Constitution, to function in the best interests of the United States of America. Adhering to this obligation and oath has never been more important.

An impeachment trial is to protect the country, not a political party, not a political agenda. Senators should conduct a fair trial under the Constitution. But will they?

Senators appealed to voters and promised that they would function in the best interest of the country as well as those who put them in office. One might ask, "What should a Senator do when there is conflict in upholding what is in the best interest of the country vs. the interest of many of the voters who elected him or her?"

That seems to be the dilemma that some of the senators face as we watch the impeachment trial of President Donald J. Trump unfolds. When such a conflict occurs, the senator should obey the Constitution and do what is in the best interest of the country as a whole.

There may be others who might disagree with this conclusion. They may feel that senators first and foremost are obligated to the people who voted for them or contributed to their campaigns. If the majority believes in a fundamental premise of our democratic form of government, then the senators should do everything in their power to find out the facts to make the right decision.

Contrary to what most people might think, an impeachment trial is to protect the country, not the president. The trial has come about because of the alleged wrong doings by the president against the well-being of the country.

What can you do for those senators that seem to be wavering? You can call, and text your senators repeatedly and tell them that the impeachment trial is to protect the country. And their obligation is to conduct a fair and factual trial irrespective of their party affiliation. The Republican Party nor the Democratic Party is on trial. The impeachment trial is to protect the country, first and foremost. Not a political party, nor a person.

In conducting the impeachment trial, not only does the validity of the United States Constitution and the well-being of the country hang in the balance, so do the patriotism, honesty, and honor of each senator.

USING MY WORD POWER

The current impeachment trial is to protect the country, not President Donald J. Trump, nor members of the Senate.

Published January 29, 2020
https://janicesellis.com

Republican Party Has Lost Its Way and Identity

The Republican Party has lost its way and identity. Will the real Republican Party please stand up? Should anyone respond to that question, who would it be? President Donald Trump and his so-called base? The Tea Party enthusiasts who were successful in 2010 in getting elected Congressmen who self-identify as neo-conservatives on one end of the spectrum and libertarians on the other end?

The Republican Party has lost its way and identity because on any given issue, one faction seems unable to control the debate. No faction can seem to win when it comes to a path forward, and therefore there is perpetual gridlock, and nothing of substance gets accomplished.

It is a party that is divided against itself and is in danger of self-destruction. No one would have imagined that the "crabs in a barrel" would be an accurate description of a political party that once boasted of being the "Party of Lincoln." Abraham Lincoln must be tumbling in his grave. I would imagine that more recent Republican Presidents, Dwight Eisenhower, even Richard Nixon, Gerald Ford, and Ronald Reagan, must be tumbling too.

What has happened to their party? The Republican Party has lost its way and identity.

Nothing provides more evidence than the current political environment. The Republican Party is in charge of the White House, the U.S. Senate, and the U.S Congress, even most state government. But which faction of the party is in charge? It appears neither because nothing is getting done, except an exchange of name calling, finger pointing, blame, invectives, and insults, while policy efforts are left in confusion and in ruin. Meanwhile, the public is caught in the lurch and the issues they care about remain unresolved.

Has the U.S. Government ever been in such disarray, such dysfunction? A house divided against itself shall not stand. Not my words, but those of the good book. But, the grave concern is, the Republican Party will not be the only one to suffer. The direction and well-being of the country is at stake.

Will the real Republican Party get its act together, stand up, and move the country forward?

Published October 6, 2017
https://janicesellis.com

Republicans Have Themselves to Blame

Republicans have themselves to blame for the rise of Donald Trump and Ted Cruz as representatives of their party and leaders in the nomination for the Republican nominee for President of the United States.

It really did not just start with this election cycle. It started with their silence about or embrace of the Tea Party element of their party, which came to power during the 2008 presidential election cycle, which President Barack Obama was victorious. Republican have themselves to blame for the emergence and success of, the extreme and often irresponsible politics of, Donald Trump and Ted Cruz. There are many party leaders and voters who share their views.

The last seven years of the Obama administration have been a consistent show of obstructionist politics by the Republican-controlled Congress that has a large contingent of Tea Party members, sympathizers, and other conservative zealots. Even the Republican Speaker of the House, John Boehner could not convince or coral a Republican-controlled House into acting or voting responsibly on legislation that even previous Republican administrations had put forth.

The marching orders of the day seem to be, since the election of President Barack Obama, oppose any and everything Obama puts forth, whether it is good for the country or not.

Republicans have themselves to blame.

Remember Republican Senate Majority Leader, Mitch McConnell, declaring that his number one goal was to defeat President Obama, make him a one-term president. He made that declaration in 2008, even before he became the Majority Leader, and he has held true to that goal, despite Obama's election for a second term. Look at McConnell's, and other Republican Senators' reactions to an Obama appointment of a Supreme Court nominee to replace the late Justice Antonin Scalia.

Call it racism. Call it conservatism. Call it what you will. But the climate during the last seven years has given rise to extremists like Donald Trump and Ted Cruz and Republicans have themselves to blame. The anti-Obama sentiment has morphed into anti-Republican establishment. They are being forced to drink their own poisonous potion.

The Republican leadership unleashed or allowed racist and extremist views to flourish. They actually threw the rock, sometimes hiding their hand, and at other times pretending that they did not see or recognize a rock had indeed been thrown. Now do you feel and see that what you allowed to go unchecked is hurting the very essence and future of the Republican Party?

Republicans themselves are to blame for the state in which they find themselves in the 2016 Presidential Election. How will you stop it?

Published March 23, 2016
https://janicesellis.com

The Obsession With Repealing Obamacare

The obsession with repealing Obamacare, the Affordable Healthcare Act, borders on a form of selective psychosis. The real question: What is the underlying cause of this seven-year+ effort to undo what has been a means to provide millions of Americans health care coverage? The continuous failed attempts are beginning to appear psychotic.

Why the obsession with repealing Obamacare when the proposed replacements will make Americans worse off? Is that sane or rational? What kind of sense does it make? Why are Republicans hell bent on repealing Obamacare?

Is it racial hatred—they just find it unacceptable that President Barack Obama, black and a Democrat, managed to pass legislation to expand health care coverage when his predecessors were unable to?

Is it the strong disdain and distaste for the most vulnerable among us—poor whites and minorities—that policymakers and their wealthy supporters feel are underserving of good health care services?

Is it the love of money, the power elite, who will tolerate and find acceptable any and all manner of inhumanity in order to preserve their wealth? It seems they find it totally acceptable to take away needed health care from some, and totally deny affordable and accessible health care to others—those who most need it, the poor the elderly, children—if they think it is going to cost them more tax dollars.

The obsession with repealing Obamacare defies logic, is inhumane, and flies in the face of how a governing body arrives at good and reasonable public policy.

Obamacare, the Affordable Healthcare Act, is not perfect. But instead of spending seven years, and counting, trying to undo it, why haven't there been efforts to improve it, fix it? Talking about throwing out the baby with the bathwater….what blind and misguided rage. It borders on psychosis.

The obsession with repealing Obamacare has occupied President Donald Trump, a Republican, before and since he took office, and both houses of this Republican Congress. What defies common sense even more are the proposals to replace Obamacare, which are draconian and worse. Why penalize and put at risk those Americans who currently have healthcare under the Affordable Healthcare Act, Obamacare? Why not fix and improve Obamacare so more Americans can receive needed health care services? That would be good public policy.

Every rational, caring Americans must be asking, "Why?" The obsession with repealing Obamacare can only confirm the hatred and disdain associated with race and poverty, and the misguided notion that government is supposed to provide and protect the well-being of the rich, not the majority of its citizenry.

The cause for the obsession with repealing Obamacare cannot be mistaken.

Published December 22, 2020
https://janicesellis.com

The Congress Christmas Song: Oh, You'd Better Watch Out....

When I look at the behavior of Congress during this last year—failure to pass the American Jobs Bill, now failure of the Super Committee to arrive at much-needed cuts in the federal budget—voters should take a lesson from Ole' Saint Nick as he prepares his sleigh with presents to be delivered for Christmas. Members of Congress certainly have not been "good for goodness sake."

Christmas is coming for every member of Congress on November 2, 2012. So, to each of them, "You'd better watch out, because voters are going to the polls." It is just unfortunate that their Christmas does not come in December as well.

But, come November, voters will do well to remember whether their congress person was sleeping or awake when it came to acting on or passing some of the most important pieces of legislation that would have improved the plight of Americans and the long-term wellbeing of America.

If they haven't already, voters truly need to assess whether Congress has been "good or bad" as they have carried out the people's business. Each voter should be "making a list, right now, and "checking it twice" to find out who has been "naughty or nice." Check the record. Time, and time again, members of Congress have chosen to be "naughty" rather than "nice."

But this "tongue and cheek" analysis aside, you get the point.

Why should we reward some members of this Congress with another term in office just so they can simply continue to *not* represent the people who put them there?

During these tough economic times, the people have made it clear, time, and time again, that they want Congress to get our fiscal house in order by reducing the deficit and our long-term debt with a combination of spending cuts and increases in taxes for those who can afford it most. Yet, this Congress continues to ignore that directive by failing to come up with reductions in spending and needed changes in the tax code.

Many Americans are hurting because of high and sustained unemployment rates. Many have lost their homes, exhausted their savings, and living a day-to-day existence because of it. President Obama developed and proposed the American Jobs Bill that had measures that were bi-partisan (many proposed by previous Republican administrations) and consistent with the goals of not increasing the deficit or long-term debt. But Congress continues in its adamant way of not even seriously considering it, even though polls consistently show that the American people support the passing of the Jobs bill.

Every serious voter has to be asking him or herself, what is causing such intransience, such vitriol, such determination, such refusal to do those things that could make things better for the American people, and thus, America.

Is it just plain old partisan politics? Is it deep subliminal and blatant racism because America has a black president, and they want him to fail? Is it greed at the corporate and individual level, where the rich want to protect their wealth at all costs? Or is it some combination of the above?

Irrespective of the reasons, each member of the public has one great present in his or her bag when Christmas rolls around for each Congressman next November—a vote. While the majority of the public may not be individually wealthy or powerful, there is a kind of power in numbers than can be more effective than money.

Americans need to determine whether they are going to reward these members of Congress for their behavior. Kids understand the concept when it comes to anticipating and wishing for presents during Christmastime. Certainly, the "adults" in Congress understands the same concept of reward and punishment during election time.

We all will have a chance to become Santa in November of 2012. Are you making a list? And, when you take a cursory review of the behavior of many, is there even a need to check it twice?

Per chance, if there is a behavior change as the November 2012 election approaches, shame on us if we forget that we have suffered needlessly, months on end, because of the performance of a Congress, which persists in acting inept and being controlled by self-interest.

Christmas is coming for Congress. Unfortunately, it is not soon enough.

Published November 22, 1011
USAonRace.com

To Impeach or Not to Impeach Is the Question

To impeach or not to impeach is the question of critical importance in the coming weeks and will be defining about what kind of nation we will be and will become. The stakes are just that high. The future character, values, and principle of our foundational institutions are hanging in the balance.

Our nation is about to embark on a defining moment, with lasting implications. The United States Senate, in accordance with the U.S. Constitution, will soon begin the impeachment trial of President Donald J. Trump. Sadly, and unfortunately, the most grave and grievous trial for this nation is being marred by lies instead of truths, gross misrepresentations instead of factual data, and hardline partisanship instead of reasonable and civil bipartisanship.

All of this morass puts the chances of arriving at the right verdict, the right outcome for the county and its citizens at risk. To impeach or not to impeach is the question. Why do we find ourselves in this muck and mire at what could be the most defining moment of this decade, if not this century, if not for the future type of government that define America?

USING MY WORD POWER

How did we get here at this critical moment in our history? The answer to this question will likely spun many answers, depending on one's political leanings, who and what one believes, and whether one is attending and carefully listening. The actions and signs have been apparent for months and years.

We all share in the responsibility, in some way, for being where we are. We have either been parties and participants to the lies, misrepresentations, and the utter disregard of our laws and institutional values. Or, we have sat idly by and watched it unfold in front of us, in some shape or fashion, almost on a daily basis and did nothing. Some may have tried to intervene. Now, we are here. To impeach or not to impeach is the question.

Perhaps, some of us have bothered to try to keep truth, facts, and integrity in the forefront as we discussed, analyzed the words and actions of President Trump. Perhaps, we have called, written, and/or texted the people we voted into office, pleading with them to put partisanship aside and do the right thing for this country and its citizens.

One thing is certain. Each of us citizens who is old enough and eligible to vote fall within one of the three groups. We are either part of the problem, have been trying to bring about a good solution, of have chosen to sit on the sidelines, not get involve, wring our hands, or simply complain.

Well, we are here. To impeach or not to impeach is the question. What are you prepared to do as the impeachment trial of President Donald J. Trump unfolds? Listen intently. Demand that your elected officials do the factual, impartial, and right things.

We all can do something, during the trial and following the trial.

Published January 12, 2020
https://janicesellis.com

Toward a More Diverse Peace Corps

A goal to have a more diverse Peace Corps in the future has been announced as it seems that the Corps in its current state does not reflect the changing face of America.

We may recall that the Peace Corps is an initiative of President John F. Kennedy. The idea was presented at the University of Michigan at Ann Harbor while he was campaigning for President. He issued a challenge to students to dedicate two years of their lives to help serve under and un-developed nations in the world.

Since its inception, the Peace Corps has sent over 200,000 young volunteers to over 130 countries throughout the world. They provide services in the areas of health, education, technology, farming, environmental management, etc.

The leadership of the Peace Corps, in announcing the goal to recruit more minorities, said it will simplify the application process and offer more incentives for students to sign on. Let us hope that in the weeks, months, perhaps years to come, that the Peace Corps' well-meaning goal will not be caught up in the same distorted morass as Affirmative Action.

The Corps plans to aggressively recruit in more racially and ethnically diverse communities. Regional recruitment offices are hiring dedicated diversity recruiters to achieve its goals.

Given the high unemployment rates among minorities, both high school and college graduates, service in the Peace Corps could prove to be a welcomed and beneficial opportunity. It could provide valuable experience and provide career paths.

The effort to get the Corps to be more reflective of the multi-racial and multi-cultural nation in which we are becoming is part of a broader initiative to make the organization more relevant and ready for the times in which we live. Toward that end, the Corps is also revamping their training and safety protocols and procedures to reflect a changing world environment, which includes terrorism.

Minorities, in addition to being desired in the Corps, will also benefit from the partnership agreement that the Corps has entered into with the University of Michigan. Students can combine Peace Corp services with graduate degrees. What a great opportunity to earn a graduate degree, receive scholarships, earn academic credits, and receive stipends as they complete their tour of service.

New recruits will have more latitude in selecting the country and area of services in which they would like to be assigned.

The Peace Corps should be commended for efforts to recruit and select more minorities to participate in the service, which could be mutually beneficial in so many ways as they put shoulder to shoulder to improve the conditions in many parts of the world that need it most.

Published May 15, 2014
https://janicesellis.com

Trump Is Many Americans' Alter Ego

Is Donald Trump many Americans' alter ego? Many pundits, policy makers and other people generally are talking about Donald Trump's meteoric rise in the polls among GOP voters and likely non-GOP voters alike.

Why has Trump managed to appear on the political landscape and seize the stage among Republican Presidential hopefuls?

Many would like to say it is because of his celebrity status. Trump, similar to Ronald Reagan, has long been on America's theatrical playground – whether with his signature real estate holdings, his flamboyant lifestyle, from marring beauty queens to hosting America's most recognized beauty pageants.

While he has had a ten-year presence in many American homes with his TV reality show, The Apprentice, where he is most remembered by his famous invective, "You are fired," many would say, even with that and his other theatrical credits, he is no Ronald Reagan.

But is he?

Ronald Reagan, like many of his cinematic roles, was seen as sort of the great cowboy riding in on the great white horse to set America straight, if indeed, not outright save her. Ronald Reagan was also labeled the great communicator.

Donald Trump, the multi-billion self-made billionaire rides in on modern day multi-media to make America great again. Trump can also be labeled if the great communicator, certainly the unbridled communicator.

Whether the analogy of being like Reagan holds or not, Trump has hit a cord with many Americans. He seems to have the knack to express in public what many Americans are feeling but will only say among family and the closest of friends or not utter at all.

Are people tired of political correctness when it comes to what really needs to be done when it comes to tough issues like immigration, the homeland war on terror, gun legislation, and many other important issues facing this country, and for which the next president will need to provide leadership?

Maybe it is not Trump's celebrity or his uncensored communication style at all that is appealing to many voters.

Maybe, it is the thought that he, because of his individual wealth, cannot be unduly influenced by lobbyists, political make-up artists and strategists who the people believe really call the shots—during the election process and well after the election is over—not the people. The peoples will seem to always fall victim to the purse strings.

Many Americans may have grown tired of being promised one thing by a candidate on the campaign trail only to get something else once he or she gets in office.

But there is one other possibility. Donald Trump's boldness, brashness, apparent courage, and apparent love of what America "use to be" represent the traits of many of America's founding fathers. They, too, were bold, said and did many things – right or wrong, justified or not, compassionate, or brutal – all in the name of building a strong America.

Donald Trump as many Americans alter ego may describe the phenomenon occurring in the 2016 Presidential Election.

Comfort can be found in the fact that the founding fathers did not like nor appreciate or tolerate tyranny at the expense of individual rights and freedom. That still remains a part of most Americans DNA, our ego.

A tyrant, in any disguise may win the Whitehouse. It is very unlike he or she will be able to rule.

Published July 29, 2015
https://janicesellis.com

Trump Hurls Insults Instead of Debating

Trump hurls insults instead of debating the issues with his opponents. This continually overshadows any substantive discussions about the 2016 Campaign for President of the United States of America. We have hit a historical and all time low in electoral politics. This is not the kind of history we as a nation, the leader of the free world, need to be making. Will rational voters please stand up?

Donald Trump has managed to become the presumptive nominee of the Republican Party for the President of President of the United States by spewing a litany of lies, insults and other actions instead of substantive discussions of issues. There are many issues looming large regarding the future well-being of our country here at home and our position and role on the world stage.

Mr. Trump managed to prevail and leave in his wake sixteen rivals, most of whom had more substantive and realistic experience in governing and more rational positions about the issues we confront. Trump hurls insults instead of debating issues, and this has propelled him to victory. He has not provided any *realistic* policy proposals to back up any of the things that he claims he will do. Will this tactic work against Hillary Clinton in the general election?

Instead, Mr. Trump has seized on many American's penchants for bigotry, fear, sexism, and racism. And do not forget the drama, entertainment, and the "reality TV" aura that surrounds him and holds a great percentage of the population sway. Trump hurls insults instead of debating. It seems to be the great attraction.

It is akin to a feeding frenzy mentality. His voters' blind and unquestioning support of him is reminiscent of the behavior of an occult. While reluctant to draw an analysis between Trump and the likes of a Jim Jones, David Koresh, or Hitler, it is hard to avoid when you listen to his spokespersons try to explain away his statements and behavior. Rational thinking seems to be non-existent.

The fact that Trump makes contradictory statements about issues, outright lies about himself and others, false accusations, and blatant disrespect seem not to matter. Even admitting that he did and said whatever it took to be successful in winning the primary election but would change and become more presidential during the general, does not seem to faze his supporters.

Who is the real Donald Trump? Do those who are voting for him really care?

USING MY WORD POWER

When Trump hurls insults instead of debating the issues rule, how can you know what he would do, and how he would do it, should he become President of the United States of America?

To whom will he be accountable?

Published December 22, 2020
https://janicesellis.com

Donald Trump, Truth, and Consequences

One could argue that "Donald Trump," "truth," and "consequences" are words that do not belong in the same sentence, same conversation, and sadly in any realm of accountability.

We are in a most unusual political season where the Republican Party's front runner for President of the United States of American can get away with almost saying anything, whether factual and truthful or not. That is for starters. Much of what Trump says is not only far from being the truth, much of it is also delivered in the most offensive and obtrusive way possible.

Mr. Trump's untruthful claims and invectives are recklessly spoken with no apparent real consequences. He continues to lead in the polls. Have you seen his boisterous declarations *vigorously* challenged by anyone in the media, during forums, during his rallies, and rare meeting with the press Corp? Some political pundits with allegiance to or alliances with other candidates may cry foul immediately following Trump's ridiculous statements, but even their cries fade.

When he declares "Things are terrible in America," is he asked for examples and the facts that support them?

USING MY WORD POWER

Why isn't he brought to task when he claims illegal immigrants are "rapists, criminals, and the Mexican government is deliberately sending them to America?" Where is his proof? Not only does Mr. Trump not present any evidence to support his claims, but he also boldly repeats them.

What about the latest claim that he saw thousands of Arab Americans celebrating in New Jersey in the aftermath of the terrorist attack on 911?

Donald Trump is leading the Republican candidates for President of the United States. What does this say about the people who are showing unwavering support for him? Do facts, truth, temperance, and respect have a place in their value set? If not, the future political direction of this great nation is on a perilous and slippery slope should Donald Trump succeed in becoming the Republican nominee for President of the United States.

What does that say about the composition, political direction, and future of what was once the Grand Ole Party? If this is where the GOP has devolved, it is surely on life support, and either need life-saving measures or be allowed to die, and a New Republican Party (NRP) to be born and blossom in its place.

From Abraham Lincoln to Ronald Reagan, what has happened to the Republican Party during the last decade must be a painful thing to watch even from the grave.

Donald Trump who runs loose with the truth, with little or no negative consequences, who spews personal insults against his fellow opposing Republican contenders and members of the press core alike is leading the pack.

How can a Trump win possibly make America great again, as his campaign slogan proclaims?

Donald Trump, truth, and consequences. He says anything and gets away with it.

Published November 23, 2015
https://janicesellis.com

Partisanship Trumps Public Policy

When partisan politics prevails, good public policy that would provide for and protect the best interests of the people is defeated and it diminishes all of America. With the gridlock that has defined the relationship of the Obama Administration and the 113th Congress, one would think that things will change when the new 114th Congress convenes in January.

But based on what appears to be intransient partisan positions, the American people may be in for more of the same: partisan politics that results in inaction and trumps the passage of good public policy.

Will there be real immigration reform legislation passed during the term of the 114th Congress?

A bi-partisan bill passed the U.S. Senate many month ago that was never brought to the floor of Congress for a vote, up or down, modification or anything?

Is that behavior doing the business of the people who elected them in the first place?

Then there is The Affordable Health Care Act, known as Obamacare. There seems to be a partisan goal to repeal it, even after more than ten million Americans, most of whom have never had health insurance now do. Why is there an obsession to repeal rather than make amendments to make it better?

Then there are the all-important issues of raising the minimum wage to help working families earn a decent wage, revising the tax codes to make them fairer and more equitable.

Great leaders, whether found in the President, a Senator, or member of the House of Representatives, know firsthand that the pathway to achieving effective public policy when the stakes are very high, and the country is in a state of crisis, is compromise.

Every major crisis this country has faced, at the end of the day, required a willingness of elected officials to sit around the table in earnest and work toward arriving at the best solution given the circumstance. But partisanship trumps public policy in the 113th Congress. Will it in the 114th?

A willingness to follow that pathway, which is replete with examples of how it has worked in both recent and distant history, will be required to pass important legislation when it comes to immigration reform, improving The Affordable Care Act, increasing the minimum wage, and revising the tax code.

Do we have any reason to expect that the new 114th Congress will work with Obama administration to compromise and pass legislation on these critical issues or any others?

If the partisan grandstanding that has followed the mid-term elections continues, then there is little reason to be optimistic. This is what happens when partisanship trumps public policy.

Published December 22, 2020
https://janicesellis.com

Show Real Patriotism by Voting

Not voting on next Tuesday, November 5, will be tantamount to being anti-democratic. At a bare minimum, it certainly can be considered half-patriotic.

Anti-democratic because in not voting we ignore one of the basic tenets of our democracy, and we abdicate one of our major responsibilities. Failing to vote essentially says that perpetuating government by the people through elected representatives is not a priority.

Instead of strengthening the power of the voice of the people, not voting weakens it.

Half-patriotic? Being a patriot means more than waving the flag and singing "God Bless America." If you love, support and are willing to defend this country and our way of life—and that is what being patriotic means—then taking time to vote is the least investment one can make.

Under normal circumstances if anyone accused us of being anti-democratic or the least bit unpatriotic, we would be at a minimum offended. With all that we have suffered as a nation over the last year, we could easily become indignant, maybe even come to blows with the accuser.

But just how deep is our love for this republic is a question well worth asking when we continually, despite the internal and external threats to it, go down this slippery slope of apathy and disinterestedness around who ultimately gets chosen to make important decisions on our behalf about the well-being and future of city, state and country.

We face some of the closest races in recent history. Every eligible voter needs, and should want, to be counted. It begs the questions what will it take to engage the non-voter.

During the last week of an election, much of the attention from candidates has traditionally focused on the undecided voters. But something needs to be done to prick the conscience of the non-voters. Non-voters have become comfortable being non-entities, being AWOL when it was time for their positions to be counted.

If one listens to the dialogue, there are growing reasons to be alarmed. There was a time when non-voters would be too ashamed to admit they did not vote or were not registered. But registered and non-registered voters, alike, seem to be comfortable expressing futility in bothering to become engaged in the political process.

They proclaim their non-participation with comfort and ease often wearing it as a badge of non-patriotic honor. You can almost hear their pious boastings: "All politicians are crooks or incompetent. Politics is no longer an honorable profession."

Show Real Patriotism by Voting

Brash, non-voting braggarts, too many of us have become.

Too many young people offer frivolous reasons for not being engaged in the electoral process. They irreverently characterize politics as boring, irrelevant or uninteresting. Many older people hide behind cynicism, finding fault, placing blame as solace is found in self-righteous indignation and the ignoble position of being a nonvoter.

The easiest thing in the world is to remain on the sidelines. Complain about how bad the candidates are when you have not bothered ask one question, attend one forum or passed out one leaflet on anyone's behalf. It is easy to stay at home or pass by the polls on voting day. It is easy to watch the returns out of curiosity to see who happened to have won. It is easy, and a popular pastime, to spend the next months and years complaining about what the elected official are doing or not doing.

There are seven days left to decide whom you will vote for Governor of Kansas, U.S. Senator from Missouri, and other state and congressional seats for both Missouri and Kansas. Candidates for these offices present clear and distinct choices. If you think there is no difference between Kathleen Sebelius and Tim Shallenberger, Jean Carnahan and Jim Talent, Adam Taff and Dennis Moore, and other candidates, you are truly out of touch with what is in the best interest of this country, your state, and your community.

So are you just a feel good, flag-waving patriot, full of bravado at the very thought of a present or imminent

USING MY WORD POWER

affront or assault on our democratic way or life? Or, are you a builder and preserver of this great republic?

Actions speak louder than words _ in the political process, too.

Published October 28, 2002
The Kansas City Star

Your Vote Is a Terrible Thing to Waste

Who will you vote for on Tuesday, November 5?

We have some very important elections taking place this year. Where are you on the candidates and the issues? What is the profile of the man or woman who potentially could represent you in Jackson County, Jefferson City and Washington? Do you really know the candidates and their stand on issues that will impact your life, members of your family, your neighborhood, your city, for the next two to six years?

Take time in the next few days to find out and cast your voice accordingly.

Your involvement and vote this Tuesday will determine the outcome for many critical offices. To name them by category gives you an idea of how much is at stake and up for grabs. The important question is: "For whom will you cast a vote when it comes to selecting a U.S. Senator from Missouri, Governor of Kansas, County Executive, State Representatives, U.S Congressman/woman and other key positions?

To understand all the issues at the county, state and federal level which will impact you and your community, I must admit, can be daunting, if not indeed overwhelming.

USING MY WORD POWER

I think it is a bit much to ask the average citizen who is preoccupied with daily issues of making ends meet, raising a family, keeping a job, to then turn around and become expert on the details on public policies or every piece of legislation. However, there are ways we can achieve a "comfort zone" around who can best represent us.

Perhaps, you might find this approach helpful as you try to get your hands around all the offices and the candidates seeking them.

1) Take a moment to reflect on one or two issues that are important to you whether they are economic development, community revitalization, jobs for youth, quality health care or some other concern.

2) Take the particular issue(s) and develop a score card on paper or in your mind and see how you, and more importantly the community or City has fared. Ask yourself the famous question: "Are you better off than you were two, three or four years ago?

Many of the issues and conditions impacting the Afro-American community here in Kansas City are the same for the city at large. Many are different. But the important thing, irrespective of the issue, is how are they dealt with and what are the attendant results short-term and long-term by the people you vote to put in office. You only have to look at a few critical indicators to reach some rather poignant conclusions:

- What do you see when you look at the state of housing in your community?

- Do you and your neighbor have access to quality health care services at prices you can afford?

- While the city and country boast of low unemployment rates, do you see the same low rates in your community? If not, why not?

- Do you see strong economic development?

- Do you have ready and convenient access to services such as a good grocery store, pharmacy, auto services, etc.?

- Is your community in a state of decline or revitalization?

- What role has each candidate played or not played on the state of our schools and the quality of education our children are receiving.

You want to find out what actions did the incumbents take or fail to take on issues they could have directly impacted. Ask the challenger for his or her specific plan to address some of the issues that are near and dear to you. When you tally your scorecard, what are your conclusion about the incumbent and the challenger?

Government and the representatives we put there will work when we insist they do with our vote and vigil. If you want to elect a U.S. Senator and U.S. Congressman, and other elected officials, who are responsive to your issues and needs, vote on Tuesday, November

USING MY WORD POWER

5 and hold the elected official accountable throughout his/her term.

Vote on who you think is the best person for the job. Tell a neighbor, a family member, or a colleague who you think will be best for your family, your neighborhood, your city, your country.

Good government, like a good family, a good church, a good school, takes having the right people at the top making good decisions. But they also take the rest of us to play our part.

Do not be content leaving the quality of your life up to someone else.

Published June 19-25, 1998
The Kansas City Globe

Will the Republican Party Recover?

Will the Republican Party recover from the anti-establishment campaign of Donald Trump, which has left it fractured and impotent? Trump has managed to become the party's presumptive nominee by running to the extreme right of many of the "public stances" the party has adhered to for generations. That is on the days that he is not sending signals that is changing positions as he goes.

For the most part, Trumps positions have been extreme in one way of the other, not unlike many of those that the party has advocated within its ranks for decades. Otherwise, how was Trump able to woo and win most Republican voters during the primary contests. Now the party has been thrown into great turmoil. Will the Republican Party recover, or will a new party emerge?

Let us take a closer look at a few of the party's stances that actually provided the impetus for Trump's ascendency.

For decades, the party has not made a concerted and effective effort to welcome and embrace minorities. Neither has Trump during the primary elections. As a matter of fact, Mr. Trump has said and done everything he could to further alienate minorities.

For decades, the party has not been pro-women in advocating for equal pay or personal control over their bodies. Neither has Donald Trump, depending on which day you ask him. If he is not insulting women, he is saying they should be punished for having an abortion.

Republican leaders in both Houses of Congress have not been pro-immigration reform to try and come up with a reasonable solution for the eleven million plus undocumented immigrants who live and work within our borders. Neither has Mr. Trump. He plans to build a wall between the U.S and Mexico, round up and deport the eleven million immigrants.

"Public stances" is the operative phrase. It brings to mind the age-old question that we often think about, if not ask, "how deep is your love?" Just how committed were members of the Republican party to widening the party's tent to include minorities of every hue and shade? How committed was the party in finding a path forward for the long-standing immigration issue? limited government, limited taxes, and conservative social values?

Did the long-standing practices of the party create the ideal opportunity for someone like a Donald Trump to emerge and takeover. Will the Republican party recover?

Many long-standing party leaders are questioning whether Trump is a true Republican and a true conservative. A lot of voters see Trump as a conservative in the extreme and have rallied behind him.

When the stalwarts and standard-bearers of the party seem to be jumping ship by the day, not only vowing that they will not attend the party convention in June, but going a step further declaring that they will not support Trump in November?

Will the Republican Party recover in time to have a possible chance of winning in November?

Published May 10, 2016
https://janicesellis.com

Elected Officials Work for Us. What Criteria Should We Use to Hire Them?

As we pause this Labor Day, we should reflect on what the holiday means and remember that elected officials in our city, county, state, the U.S. Senate, and House of Representatives work for us, the people.

We are the employer.

What guide or criteria should we use to determine who to hire or rehire with our vote?

In the last eight weeks leading up to the midterm elections, we will be bombarded by applicants.

In addition to the many political messages dominating the airwaves — and in print and online media — many aspiring candidates will be making the rounds at public gatherings, political forums and other venues.

But beware. Shaking hands, kissing babies and making a few remarks should not be considered anything more than an initial application.

Most of us will have a lot of decisions to make about who we want to represent us in almost every level of our government.

For example: In Missouri we have Republican Eric Schmitt, Democrat Trudy Bush Valentine, Libertarian Jonathan Dine and Constitution Party Paul Venable being interviewed for the job of U.S. Senator.

All of the seats for the U.S. House of Representatives in Missouri are up for hire.

All 163 seats in the Missouri House, and half the 34 seats in the Missouri Senate, are on the ballot.

While there are unique roles and responsibilities associated with each elective office, there are certain basic and prerequisite qualifications that all candidates should hold in common.

No doubt, voters have things they look for and require of someone they are going to vote for (hire).

But here are a few qualifications that we should want in anyone seeking to be hired to lead and represent the interest of ourselves, family, community, state and nation.

First and foremost, does the candidate believe in America, our form of democracy and how it should function at the national, state and local level?

Does the candidate fully understand and embrace the responsibilities of the office they seek?

In carrying out the roles and responsibilities of the office, will the candidate perform their duties in a way that is consistent with – and promote – the stability and best results for the constituency the office represents?

When it comes to values, principles and ethics, does the candidate have a history and reputation of being honest and functioning with high integrity, have a communication style that is unifying rather than divisive, and work in a collaborative way to achieve progress in solving issues?

Those should be minimum requirements to even be considered for office.

If a candidate has held the job before, and is seeking to be rehired, there is another set of questions to be asked.

What is their record of working and voting on the issues you care about? What successes have they had; what legislation have they sponsored, supported, and passed? Have they communicated with you while they held the job? What are they proposing to do about the issues that are important to you?

For a candidate seeking public office for the first time, it is fair to ask other questions. Why are they seeking office? What is their life or professional experiences that qualifies them to seek it? What have they done to impact the lives of others, their community and the governmental office they want to represent?

As much as we may not like or see ourselves as being employers, as much as we may feel that we are already overburden with the demands of trying to keep our personal lives together and moving forward, we must take the midterm elections before us just as seriously, perhaps more seriously, than we have taken any elections.

We have applicants for important elective offices across every level of government who have divergent views, experiences and perspectives on how the role and responsibilities of the offices they seek should be carried out.

There are so many defining issues before us – election integrity, voting rights, sensible gun control, climate change, public education, immigration, the rule of law, law and order, health care access and others – that the policy decisions made will determine the quality of life in America in the near and long term.

Given these challenges along with the threats we face at every level of government in this democratic republic, we the public – the people – must rise and assume a more active and engaged role as the employer of elective government and hold who we hire accountable.

On this Labor Day, let us pause and embrace the important role we have to hire the right elected officials who have the right character, values, qualifications and commitment to get the job done in a stellar and honorable way at every level of government.

It is not enough to hire the right mayor, county executive, state senator or representative, governor, the right U.S. Senator or member of Congress. We need to hold them accountable to protect and promote a healthy, vibrant and good America across the board.

Our future well-being as a nation, as citizens, depends on it.

Published September 5, 2022
Missouri Independent.com

PostScript: Onward and Upward

My journey in becoming an advocate journalist has not been a deliberate, well-planned pursuit. There have been many converging societal and personal forces impacting my life, oftentimes, all at once it seemed. They all have determined and impacted who I have become, and the choices I have made in fulfilling what I deem as my purpose, calling, and response to this gift of life.

The sum total of my experiences—personally, professionally, educationally, economically, socially, culturally—provide the authenticity, the authority, the mission, the grist, which I think are required, and upon which I have functioned as an advocate journalist throughout my career. I have functioned as an advocate journalist while simultaneously holding positions as a government and corporate executive, a small business owner, a mayoral candidate for a major American city, a non-profit executive before becoming a full-time advocate journalist in recent years.

Continuing to be an advocate journalist still calls.

Sources

Selected articles for this book originally appeared in the following publications.

Online Publications:

JaniceSEllis.com Janice Ellis | Author | Life, Liberty, Pursuit of Happiness | Race | Gender (janicesellis.com), 2014–Present.

Missouri Independent.com Janice Ellis, Author at Missouri Independent

USAonRace.com Race Relations In The USA and Diversity News (usaonrace.com), 2007–2014

RaceReport.com Race Report, 2012–2016.

Newspapers:

Kansas City Star, 2000–2004
Kansas City Call, 2002—2007
Kansas City Globe, 1989–2007
Milwaukee Community Journal, 1983–1986
Milwaukee Business Journal, 1984—1986

USING MY WORD POWER

Radio Stations:

WISN Radio, ABC Affiliate, 1974—1976

About the Author

Janice S. Ellis, M.A., M.A., Ph.D., a native daughter of Mississippi, grew up and came of age during the height of the Civil Rights Movement and the Women's Liberation Movement. Born and reared on a small cotton farm, she was influenced by two converging forces that would set the course of her life.

The first was the fear and terror felt by Blacks because of their seeking to exercise the right to vote along with other rights and privileges afforded whites. She became determined to take a stand and not accept the limits of that farm life nor the strictures of oppressive racial segregation and gender inequality. She aspired to have and achieve a different kind of life—not only for herself but for others.

The second was her love of books, the power of words, and her exposure to renowned columnists Eric Sevareid of The CBS Evening News with Walter Cronkite and Walter Lippmann, whose column appeared for more than three decades in over 250 major newspapers across the United States and another 50 newspapers in Europe.

It was the study of Lippmann's books and commentary that inspired her to complete a Master of Arts degree in

Communication Arts, a second Master of Arts degree in Political Science, and a Doctor of Philosophy in Communication Arts, all from the University of Wisconsin. It was during her course of study that her unwavering belief—the belief that the wise use of words is what advances a good society—was solidified.

Dr. Ellis has been an executive throughout her career, first in government, then in a large pharmaceutical company, later as President and CEO of a marketing firm, and as President and CEO of a bi-state non-profit child advocacy agency. Along with those positions, she has been writing columns for nearly four decades on race, politics, education, and other social issues for a major metropolitan daily newspaper, *The Kansas City Star*; a major metropolitan business journal, *Milwaukee Business Journal*; and for community newspapers *The Milwaukee Courier*, *The Kansas City Globe*, and *The Kansas City Call*. She wrote radio commentary for two years for one of the largest ABC radio affiliates in Wisconsin and subsequently wrote and delivered a two-minute spot on the two largest Arbitron-rated radio stations in the Greater Kansas City area. She has also written for several national trade publications, focusing on healthcare and the pharmaceutical industry.

Currently, she is a columnist for the *Missouri Independent*. She has her own website, JaniceSEllis.com, which houses a collection of her writings and where she continues to write commentary.

About the Author

Dr. Ellis is the author of four award-winning books. Her most recent book, ***From Liberty to Magnolia: In Search of the American Dream – New Edition*** (2023), received great editorial reviews and continues to receive great customer reviews. It also won the 2023 Foreword Indies Book of the Year Award Silver Medal Award.

USING MY WORD POWER: Advocating for a More Civilized Society (2022), has received great editorial reviews and was a First-Place winner of the Nellie Bly Nonfiction Journalism Award. It also won the Midwest Independent Publishers Association Book Award in the Nonfiction – Social Science/Political Science/Culture category.

Shaping Public Opinion: How Real Advocacy Journalism™ Should Be Practiced (2021) won the Nellie Bly Nonfiction Journalism Award and the Gold Medal Award for nonfiction books from the Non-Fiction Author Association. It has received great national editorial reviews and continues to receive great customer reviews.

The first edition of ***From Liberty to Magnolia: In Search of the American Dream*** **(2018)** has received several national and international awards since its initial release. Among them: Independent Press Award for Race Relations (May 2020); New York City Big Book Award for Women Issues (November 2019); the Grand Prize Journey Award for Nonfiction (April 2019) from Chanticleer International Book Reviews; the Gold Medal Award for Nonfiction Books from the Non-Fiction Authors Association (May 2018), the highest award bestowed for nonfiction authors. **From Liberty to Magnolia** received a notable editorial review and honor from Kirkus Reviews, one of the oldest and most credible reviewers of books for libraries, schools, bookstores, publishers, agents, and other industry professionals. In bestowing the honor, Kirkus noted, "*From Liberty to Magnolia* was selected by our Indie Editors to be featured in *Kirkus Reviews* April 15, 2018 Issue. Congratulations! Your review has appeared as one of the 35 reviews in the Indie section of the magazine which is sent out to over 5,000 industry professionals (librarians, publishers, agents, etc.) Less than 10% of our Indie reviews are chosen for this, so it's a great honor." The book continues to receive great customer reviews.

Follow her on **Facebook Twitter Instagram LinkedIn YouTube**

www.ingramcontent.com/pod-product-compliance
Lightning Source LLC
Chambersburg PA
CBHW060451030426
42337CB00015B/1544